FLIGHT SIMULATOR
AND
FLIGHT SIMULATOR II
82 CHALLENGING
NEW ADVENTURES

FLIGHT SIMULATOR
AND
FLIGHT SIMULATOR II
82 CHALLENGING
NEW ADVENTURES
DAVE PROCHNOW

TAB TAB BOOKS Inc.
Blue Ridge Summit, PA 17214

To Kathy

FIRST EDITION
FIRST PRINTING

Copyright © 1987 by TAB BOOKS Inc.
Printed in the United States of America

Library of Congress Cataloging in Publication Data

Prochnow, Dave.
Flight Simulator and Flight Simulator II.

Includes index.
1. Flight simulators.   2. Airplanes—Piloting—
Data processing.   I. Title.
TL712.5.P746   1987   629.132′52′078   86-30113
ISBN 0-8306-0462-6
ISBN 0-8306-2862-2 (pbk.)

Contents

**Part 2
Historical Aviation Scenarios**

Preface

Leading a small, but profitable, market of home computer aero-software are three programs which represent over 90 percent of all flight simulator software sales. Remarkably, this flight trio—Flight Simulator, Flight Simulator II, and JET—are all designed by the same company, subLOGIC Corporation (whose name curiously sounds like a digital oxymoron).

One plea that has been voiced by owners of these programs centers on ideas for creative uses of this new-found computer flight ability. To a limited extent, subLOGIC has responded to this request by designing special scenery disks that allow the user to fly in different parts of the world. Unfortunately, scenery disks fail to satisfy the computer pilot's hunger for action. This book is the answer to this problem.

In its 13 chapters, this book captures all of the thrill and excitement of flight. For example, in one chapter, you'll be placed on Kill Devil Hill with the Wright Brothers for their historic flight. Later, you'll stress your flying skills to their limits with mail delivery during a raging snowstorm in 1921. Even high-performance aerobatics will be attempted in chapters dealing with special aerobatic maneuvers. No matter where a particular chapter takes you, however, the book's structure will have you successfully flying Flight Simulator to complete your assigned flight.

There is one small matter of style that will be followed throughout the remainder of this book. Instead of constantly referring to both Flight Simulator and Flight Simulator II in each software reference, only the more general Flight Simulator moniker will be used for labeling both programs. Therefore, both Flight Simulator and Flight Simulator II software owners (along with the myriad of different computer types) can ably substitute their particular version for each Flight Simulator mention.

Starting with a brief introduction to flight simulation and several instructional chapters dealing with actual computer flight, this book will launch into 82 different historical aviation scenarios for duplication with the subLOGIC Flight Simulator II and Microsoft Flight Simulator software. Each of these scenarios follows a standard presentation format. By using this consistent format, each scenario can be quickly set up by the reader and "flown" on the computer without interrupting the action through constant text references. Furthermore, once the scenario has been completed, a flight debriefing will accurately judge the Flight Simulator pilot's performance. This grading technique makes this an interactive guide and not just another mundane sightseeing tour of Flight Simulator scenery.

Concluding the book are four appendices that will enhance your overall enjoyment of the main text's aviation scenarios. Two of these appendices offer the reader valuable reference materials for dealing with the 82 scenarios. Appendix C is a complete visual identification guide to the aircraft that are presented in all 82 scenarios. Supplementing Appendix C, Appendix D provides a brief listing of significant dates in the history of aviation. This appendix will give you some idea of where a particular scenario fits into the overall fabric of aviation history.

Appendices A and B are bonuses in a book of this nature. The first of these two appendices contains thumbnail reviews of the more popular flight simulation programs that can be found in today's market. Similarly, Appendix B supplies a complete program listing for your own flight simulator. Written in several of the more popular personal home computer BASIC dialects, this appendix will give you something else to fly when you're not engaged with one of the 82 Flight Simulator scenarios.

As you race against Amelia Earhart in the 1936 Bendix Trophy Race, remember that one overriding factor separates you from the historical actions you are simulating—survivability. In other words, if you get into trouble, you can always exit Flight Simulator and restart the scenario. Where else can you climb into a multi-thousand dollar piston-powered racer, battle horrendous environmental conditions, crash your aircraft, and live to tell about it?

Acknowledgments

Four companies that provided extensive support during the preparation of this book are: Beech Aircraft Corporation, Cessna Aircraft Company, Gates Learjet Corporation, and subLOGIC Corporation. Their informational contributions helped fortify the factual accounts contained within this book.

Introduction

Many critics argue that actual flight is difficult, if not impossible, to duplicate. They will state that although microcomputer-based flight simulation software makes a strong attempt at generating the ''feel'' of flying, there are several parameters that are still beyond even the most capable computer's abilities. Continuing their case, these skeptics claim that the confinement of the cockpit, the sensation of movement, the feel of the engine's thrust, and the breathtaking beauty of aerial panoramic views serve as identifiable weaknesses in today's programming.

Balanced against these wholly negative views are the numerous merits of flight simulation programming. For example, fabulous graphics and stunning synthesized sound effects are quickly narrowing the distance between real and simulation with at least two of these previously labeled shortcomings. Actually, these differences don't have to be completely eliminated; just lessening their disparity will help to validate computerized flight simulation as being realistic. Who knows, maybe someday you will ''board'' your computer and take an imaginary vacation flight, complete with passengers.

Oddly enough, flight simulators haven't always been the exclusive domain of microcomputers. Ed Link in 1929 sparked an interest in artificial flight with the development of his first primary Link Trainer. This early effort was crude by today's standards. Only a control yoke and rudder pedals served as controls for this early flight simulator. There was also a modest number of instruments to provide the pilot with a rudimentary indication of the craft's current flight orientation. The hallmark feature of the Link Trainer, however, was its ability to move proportionately in accordance with the movement of the yoke and rudder pedals. This movable trainer is in marked contrast with the current crop of stationary simulators. In fact, the Link Trainer's simulator movement did present several technical problems. Most of these problems centered around mechanical difficulties associated with the pneumatic bellows that provided the bulk of the Link Trainer's flight characteristics.

Eventually, the Link Trainer caught the eye of a war-conscious Army Air Corps. Fueled by a desire to train pilots with a minimum of cost, the Army used an enhanced version of the Link Trainer for providing instructions to thousands of young cadets as a supplement to their Fairchild, Stearman, and Vultee flight training. The United States aerial achievements in the European and Pacific Theaters of Operations during World War II indicate the success of this fledgling flight simulation program.

Even the movable Link Trainer suffered from similar losses in realism that have been previously identified as a peculiarity of the computer-based flight simulator. Therefore, the artificial production of aircraft movements does very little in enhancing the flight simulator's realistic qualities. This leaves only the confinement of the cockpit as the final barrier preventing the acceptance of flight simulation software. For the vast majority of simulator pilots, sitting in a straight-backed chair satisfies this requirement. If, on the other hand, you share the critics' viewpoint that the claustrophobic confines of a cockpit are vital to the success of a flight simulator, then operate your computer simulator while seated inside a closet.

Recognizing the realism limitations that are imposed on flight simulation software makes the achievement of subLOGIC Corporation even more outstanding. What started as a three-dimensional graphics demonstration program in 1979 by Bruce Artwick quickly mushroomed into the most popular flight simulator ever. Flight Simulator and Flight Simulator II place the computer user inside the cockpit of a piston-powered aircraft. From this vantage point, all of the controls, operations, and actions of this aircraft are realistically simulated.

Flight Simulator and Flight Simulator II dominated the computer airways for nearly seven years. In late 1985, several new flight simulation programs started to make significant inroads into the Flight Simulator market, however (see Appendix A for reviews of these programs). Meeting this challenge, Artwick, Charles Guy, and subLOGIC released their first major new flight simulator in over six years. JET represented an enormous upgrade from the piston days of Flight Simulator. Now, the computer user was thrust into the cockpit of either a General Dynamics F-16 Fighting Falcon or a McDonnell Douglas F/A-18 Hornet. These high-performance jet aircraft stressed the very limits of current flight simulation technology.

The single catch that restricted improvements in flight simulation software was identified by subLOGIC in 1986. Graphics imaging processing needed to be enhanced for both animation speed and image resolution. A graphics card for the IBM PC, the X-1 Graphics Board, was manufactured by subLOGIC as an alternative to increasing the graphics performance of the microcomputer. A special subLOGIC support software package, 3D Graphics, complemented the X-1 Graphics Board.

Interestingly enough, the 3D Graphics software contains the same drivers that generate the animation found on JET, Flight Simulator, and Flight Simulator II. Theoretically, the next generation of flight simulation programs could come from this powerful hardware/software animation combination. The realization of this point would be indeed ironic, as subLOGIC would still be directing the path of flight simulators, but from an entirely different perspective.

Continuing the cause for realistic flight simulation software even further, subLOGIC is currently updating a thorough set of scenery disks. This scenery software is for use in conjunction with Flight Simulator, Flight Simulator II, and JET. Basically, these disks contain massive graphics databases that provide detailed ground imagery for selected areas around the world. Cities, buildings, highways, and other noteworthy landmarks are all painstakingly digitized on these scenery disks. By using these special scenery disks, the Flight Simulator II pilot can land at a detailed airport in Osaka, Japan, or JET can be flown on a high-performance mission over San Francisco Bay.

In addition to providing the scenery disks, subLOGIC is constantly translating all three of its flight simulation programs into versions that will operate on the most popular microcomputers. This translation process includes making Flight Simulator available for the Apple Computer Macintosh (Fig. I-1), the Atari 520ST and 1040ST, and the Commodore Amiga. One problem that was initially encountered with these particular translations was in adapting the user interface from a keyboard/joystick combination to a keyboard/mouse operation (Fig. I-2). The success of this modifi-

Fig. I-1. A forward view from the cockpit of the Macintosh Gates Learjet 25G Flight Simulator.

cation is best judged by taking one of these 68000-based versions of Flight Simulator up for a test flight. Following this evaluation, even the staunchest joystick jockey will find that total control is not only possible but extremely realistic through the clicking and dragging movements of the mouse.

There are three different aircraft available in Flight Simulator: a Piper PA-28-181 Archer II (found in Flight Simulator II versions only), a Cessna Skylane RG II, and a Gates Learjet LR-25G (presently found only in 68000-based Flight Simulator versions). The performance characteristics of these three aircraft make it easy for each one of them to "outfly" the simulator pilot. For this reason, an extensive training program is presented in Part I of this book. Read and understand the four chapters in this portion of the book before attempting any of the historical aviation scenarios that are discussed in Part II. Remember, only through careful training can a mission be successfully completed.

Including the Gates Learjet 25G in Flight Simulator provides the computer user with the unique opportunity to pilot one of today's most sophisticated business jets. Gone are the days of 150 knot airspeeds and limited aerobatic capability. This bizjet can climb to altitudes in excess of 50,000 feet at speeds approaching Mach .7. In fact, once you have completed your advanced aircraft training in Part I, you will be able to take off in the Gates Learjet 25G, assume an altitude of 30,000 feet, and execute several high-speed maneuvers.

These three aircraft types as used in Flight Simulator offer a smorgasbord of realistic performance specifications. Starting with the Flight Simulator II Archer II, the simulator pilot will be flying an aircraft with a 35 foot wingspan and a 23 foot 9.5 inch total length. The maximum takeoff weight for the Archer II is 2,550 pounds. Power for this aircraft comes from a single Avco Lycoming O-360-A4M four-cylinder piston engine that is capable of 180 horsepower. In flight, the

PA-28-181 can reach a maximum speed of 147 knots and an altitude in excess of 13,650 feet.

Following in a similar mold, the Skylane RG II measures 36 feet across its wings and 28 feet from nose to tail (Fig. I-3). A maximum takeoff weight of 3,100 pounds is made possible by one Continental O-470-S six-cylinder piston engine, which generates 230 horsepower. A maximum speed of 146 knots and altitudes above 14,900 feet are achievable with this Cessna.

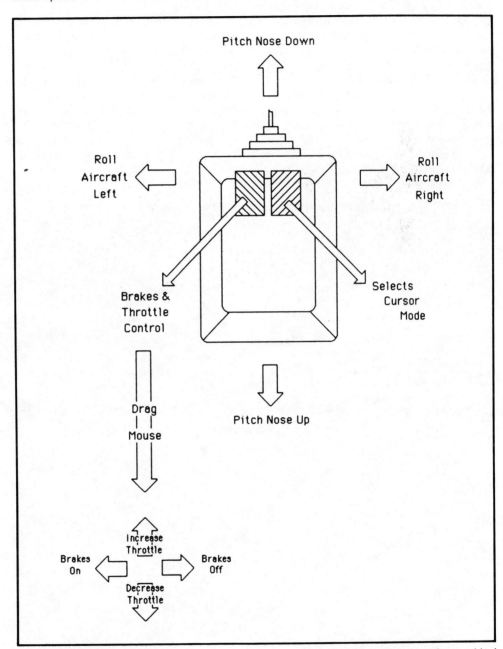

Fig. I-2. The diversity in function assigned to the Amiga mouse makes this odd user interface an ideal complement to the flight simulator.

Finally, the Gates Learjet 25G advances computer-based flight simulation into the jet age (Fig. I-4). With a wingspan of 35 feet 7.2 inches and an overall length of 47 feet 7.2 inches, the LR-25G is a sleek, high-performance aircraft. Two General Electric CJ610-8A turbofan engines provide 2,950 pounds of thrust each. The power from the combined thrust of these two engines is capable of lifting a maximum takeoff weight of 16,300 pounds. This Gates Learjet flies at a maximum speed of 464 knots and altitudes above 51,000 feet.

All of these ''real-life'' performance features are simulated through an elaborate series of cockpit instrumentation on the computer monitor. Although all of the gauges, meters, and displays which constitute the cockpit instrument panel are fairly straightforward in their function, they can be potentially disorienting on the pilot's initial Flight Simulator encounter. Taking several simulated flights will familiarize you with the use of the cockpit's instruments. Then, after you thoroughly understand the operation of the cockpit, you will be able to customize its displayed information for your particular flight. This piloting technique does require a complete mastery of the keyboard (and joystick, if you elect to use this optional element) and its associated control locations. The four chapters in Part I will provide you with all of the instruction necessary for learning the computer interface, manipulating the cockpit, and operating the control surfaces. Even if you are a veteran flier, you should complete the solo test that is found in Chapter 4 and earn your wings prior to attempting any of the 82 historical aviation scenarios depicted in Part II.

Fig. I-3. The Cessna 182 Skylane. This example is a 182K Skylane manufactured in 1967. (courtesy Cessna Aircraft Company)

Fig. I-4. The Gates Learjet 25G. The raised ribs on the wings are wing fences, which lend greater slow-speed handling capability. (courtesy Gates Learjet Corp.)

Part 1
Earn Your Wings

Chapter 1

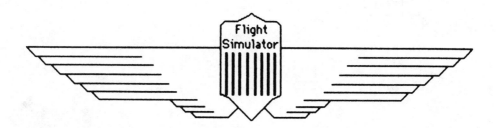

Aircraft and Computer Flight

The essence of flight is air movement. Governing the movement of this air are specific physical laws. These laws and their associated principles are the invisible forces that make an aircraft fly. Whether the air is moving around your automobile driving along the highway or speeding past the nose of a supersonic jet aircraft, the application of these laws remains identical. Adhere to these laws and the object will possess aerodynamic properties. Conversely, violate these basic physical principles and the flow of air will be disrupted and flight will be negated.

AERODYNAMICS

There are four forces that act on the aerodynamics of an object: lift, gravity, thrust, and drag. Figure 1-1 illustrates the action that these four forces exert on an aircraft in flight. By successfully juggling these four forces, *any* object can be made to fly (a whimsical extension of this statement is voiced by McDonnell Douglas F-4 Phantom II pilots, who claim that the F-4 proved the point that given enough thrust, even a brick can fly).

   Lift. *Lift*, the first of these forces, serves as the major reason that an aircraft flies. Air moving across the upper and lower surfaces of a wing produces the necessary lift for flight. When dealing with flight, lift must be strong enough to counteract the force of gravity. Therefore, in order to generate the required degree of lift, special aerodynamic features must be applied to the wing. The leading feature in making the needed lift is the *airfoil* of the wing.

   Airfoils serve two functions in generating lift on a wing: reducing turbulence and increasing the wing's upper surface distance. The reduction in turbulence is necessary for minimizing the amount of flight-destroying drag (Fig. 1-2), whereas the increased upper surface distance results in a lower atmospheric pressure for air moving over the wing. While the concept of reduced turbulence is relatively easy to grasp, the notion of a greater distance producing a lowered air pressure deserves some further elaboration.

   In the mid-1700s, a Swiss mathematician named Daniel Bernoulli postulated that the pressure of a gas decreases as the speed of the gas increases. Today, over 200 years after its discovery, Bernoulli's principle still dictates the design of airfoils. By studying the shape of a basic

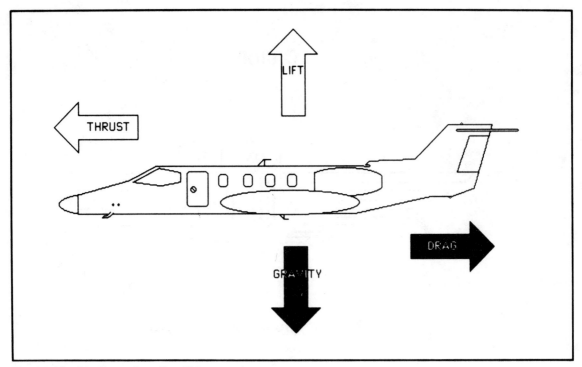

Fig. 1-1. The four forces that affect flight.

airfoil (Fig. 1-3), the full impact on lift that is made by this gas law can be visualized.

The upper surface of a wing is generally curved. This curved airfoil shape makes the distance over the wing's upper surface, from the leading edge to its trailing edge, longer than the same distance over the wing's flatter bottom surface. Due to this increased distance, air moving around this airfoil will move faster across the upper surface than across the bottom surface. This faster-moving air will create a lower air pressure over the wing's upper surface. The final result from this increased pressure underneath the wing is lift.

Several other factors can affect the total lift produced by the airfoil of a wing. Increasing the wing's angle into the moving air increases the speed of the air moving over the upper surface. In turn, this creates greater lift. The angle formed by the wing and the moving air is called the *angle of attack*. A negative lift is developed when the angle of attack is increased to a point where air "bubbles," or turbulence is produced on the wing's upper surface. This effect is known as

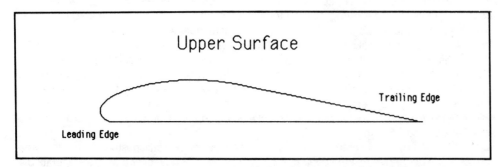

Fig. 1-2. A stylized airfoil where the leading edge is placed in the path of the air flow.

4

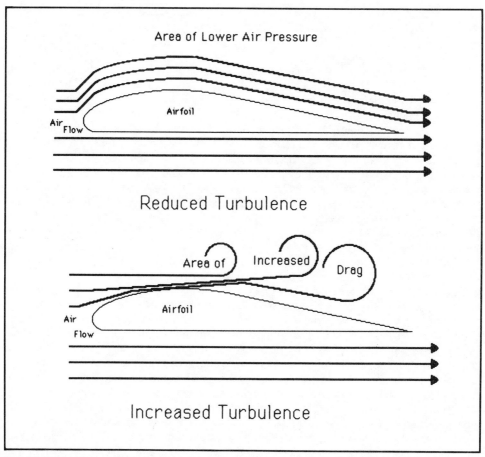

Area of Lower Air Pressure

Airfoil

Air Flow

Reduced Turbulence

Area of Increased Drag

Airfoil

Air Flow

Increased Turbulence

Fig. 1-3. Under normal flight conditions, air moves smoothly over the upper surface of an airfoil. If this flow is disrupted, however, then increased turbulence will cause drag and reduce the airfoil's lift.

a *stall*. A stall can be counteracted by another lift-producing agent—airspeed. Increased airspeeds also raise the pressure difference between the wing's upper and lower surfaces, which results in greater lift. As a rule, the square of the airspeed equals the amount of increase in lift.

One last item concerning lift deals with two control surfaces that can be attached to a wing for increased lift. A *slot* is a movable opening that is usually located along the leading edge of a wing. Using a slot delays the point at which a wing will stall. Therefore, when a slot is extended, the pilot is able to fly at a slower speed and still retain increased lift.

The other control surface is a *flap*. Flaps are downward-moving sections found along a wing's trailing edge. Lowering a flap exaggerates the curvature of the wing's airfoil. The enlarged size of the airfoil slows the speed of the aircraft, as well as increasing the wing's lift. Flaps are best used during landings. There are times, however, when the increased lift (in spite of the decreased airspeed) is desired during takeoffs.

Gravity. The negative force that fights the lift of a wing is the weight of the aircraft or the gravitational pull of the Earth. Basically, the aircraft must overcome the effects of gravity in order to fly. Once an aircraft achieves level flight, however, the combination of gravity and lift must equal zero. Otherwise, the aircraft would either drop like a rock (when gravity is greater than lift) or continually rise (if lift were greater than gravity).

5

Another important aspect of gravity is that the aircraft must possess a point where the entire weight of the plane is equally displaced. This balance point, or the *center of gravity*, for the aircraft must rest within the wing's *center of lift*. Successfully mating these two points determines the final stability and flight characteristics of the aircraft.

Generally speaking, the wing's center of lift is at a point that is one-fourth of the distance from the leading edge to the trailing edge. Bringing the center of gravity ahead of this point will result in an aircraft that is noseheavy. Likewise, placing the center of gravity behind this point produces a tailheavy aircraft.

Once the center of gravity has been correctly placed on the center of lift, the aircraft's three axes of movement can be established (Fig. 1-4). These three axes form the basis for the control of an aircraft's flight. Moving the aircraft's nose up and down rotates around the *pitch axis*. Movement around the *yaw axis* causes the aircraft's nose to travel horizontally from side to side. The last axis, the *roll axis*, represents the movement from the aircraft's wingtips being alternately raised and lowered. There are several control surfaces located on the wing and on the tail that move the aircraft around these three axes. The *elevator* handles the pitch axis. Yaw is controlled by the *rudder*. Lastly, a pair of *ailerons* control an aircraft's roll. The full effect of these three control surfaces will be more fully explained in the next section.

Only through the precise movement of these three control surfaces can an aircraft be correctly flown. Failure to master the required amount of coordination between these control surfaces can result in some unwanted flight characteristics. For example, the exclusive use of the rudder in a bank or turn produces excessive yaw. This overabundance of yaw will cause the tail of the aircraft to skid away from the turn. Similarly, relying on ailerons exclusively in a bank or turn generates too much roll. The increased roll makes the aircraft slip into the turn. One final control failure can turn into disaster: While a stall, in itself, can be a life-threatening loss of pitch control, the liberal application of rudder during a stall overloads the yaw axis and produces a tailspin. The end result from a tailspin is the almost certain loss of the aircraft. Unfortunately, the disoriented pilot will usually meet the same fate as the aircraft.

Thrust. Pushing the aircraft forward is the force of *thrust*. The thrust necessary for moving the aircraft can be produced by a number of different means. Piston engines driving propellers and turbojet turbines providing jet propulsion are the two most common methods of generating thrust. In the case of the propeller, thrust is developed by the shape of the individual propeller blades. Each blade has an airfoil shape. This airfoil, like its counterpart found in a wing, creates a region of low pressure on its upper (forward) surface and a region of higher pressure along the bottom (rear) surface. Therefore, with the propeller blade's upper surface facing away from the aircraft, the difference in air pressure on each blade forces the aircraft to move forward.

An interesting extension of the standard propeller is the *variable-pitch* propeller. This propeller is able to produce greater thrust by altering each blade's angle of attack. In order to change the propeller's pitch, the pilot merely rotates a pitch dial from inside the cockpit. Additionally, there is an extreme setting on the pitch control that places each blade parallel to the aircraft's fuselage. This condition is known as a *feathered* propeller. Feathering is usually applied to a faulty engine as a precaution against catastrophic disaster.

Countering the force of thrust is *drag*. During takeoff, thrust must be greater than drag. Once level flight is reached, however, both thrust and drag are equal. If thrust were unbridled from the negating effects of drag, the aircraft would constantly accelerate. This cancellation prevents the problems associated with continuous acceleration.

Switching from propeller thrust to jet thrust does increase the speed of the aircraft. Thrust from a jet engine differs from that produced by a propeller. With a jet engine, a reaction is produced inside the engine through the burning of fuel and the compression of air. The force of this reaction is directed out the rear of the jet engine. As this controlled combustion is expelled, the engine "reacts" by moving in the opposite direction from the exhaust.

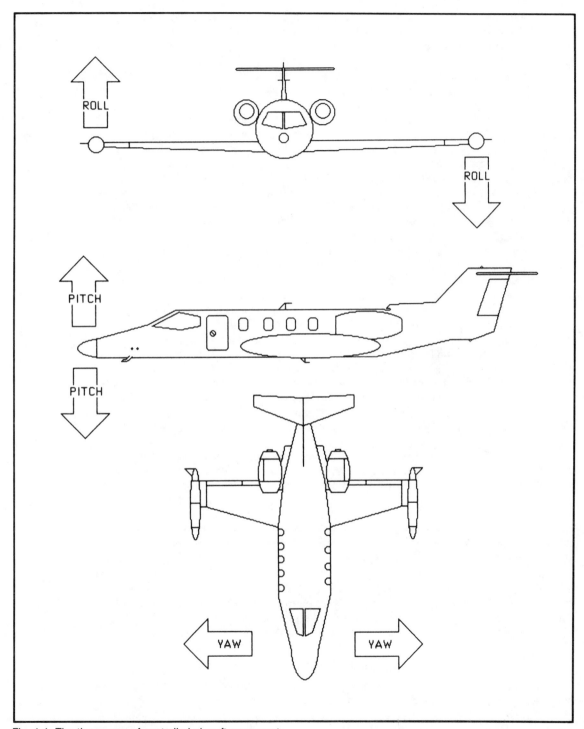

Fig. 1-4. The three axes of controlled aircraft movement.

Jet engine power is measured in *pounds of thrust*. In comparing jet thrust to propeller thrust, one horsepower is equal to one pound of thrust at 375 mph. Therefore, at lower speeds, jets offer few thrust advantages over propeller-driven aircraft. This equality differs dramatically at higher speeds. A jet engine delivering 10,000 pounds of thrust at 750 mph is equal to a 20,000-horsepower engine. Similarly, in jet engines, as thrust and airspeed increase, the total engine horsepower also increases. Conversely, physical limitations in the operation of a propeller prevent such significant horsepower production.

One important attribute of the enormous power capabilities of the jet engine is found in flying at great speeds. These great aircraft speeds can reach a point where they exceed the speed of sound. Supersonic speeds are usually expressed by a *Mach number*. Basically, Mach 1 equals the speed of sound at a given altitude. For example, sound travels at 760 mph at sea level. Therefore, an aircraft traveling at 760 mph would be moving at Mach 1 at this altitude. By increasing altitude, however, it is also possible to increase the Mach number without increasing the airspeed (due to sound's decreased speed at higher altitudes). In other words, an aircraft going 760 mph at 40,000 feet has a Mach number of 1.15. Comparing these two examples, it is easy to see how the exclusive use of the Mach number can cause confusion (e.g., 874 mph at sea level equals Mach 1.15). Combining a reference altitude with each Mach value eliminates this arbitrariness.

Drag. Negating the effects of thrust is the force of drag. Every air disturbance generated by the aircraft produces drag. This disturbance can be caused by the fuselage, canopy, and even rivets in the skin of the aircraft. Special streamlining techniques are used to minimize the production of drag. Even an aerodynamically clean aircraft still creates drag.

Skin friction is the leading cause of drag. Basically, the layer of air next to the aircraft's skin rubs against the air moving by the aircraft, which results in friction. There are two flow patterns exhibited by the movement of air between these two layers: *laminar flow* and *turbulent flow*. Laminar flow is a smooth flow of air that is generally found on the forward portion of an aircraft. An aircraft surrounded by laminar flow would have very little drag. As the air moves along the surfaces of the aircraft, however, it increases in both turbulence and friction. This movement of air is called turbulent flow. Minimizing the formation of turbulent airflow is the best method of reducing skin friction and drag.

A technique known as *boundary-layer control* helps in preventing the development of turbulent airflow. Special porous aircraft skins, along with high-pressure vacuum pumps, help to smooth out turbulent airflow patterns. Forestalling the occurrence of turbulent flow keeps an aircraft's drag to a minimum. A fringe benefit of boundary-layer control when applied to the upper surface of an aircraft's wing is that it can also reduce a wing's ability to stall. This reduced stall capability gives an aircraft greater low-speed handling and increased takeoff and landing performance.

When dealing with jet aircraft, an additional form of drag is possible. Flying at supersonic speeds violently disturbs the surrounding air, causing a shock wave. This shock wave raises the drag of the aircraft. The increased drag of supersonic flight is offset by higher jet engine thrust and the employment of area-rule principles in design. The *area-rule principle* is a special supersonic aircraft feature in which the fuselage becomes narrower at the wing attachment point (Fig. 1-5). This slight indentation of the fuselage results in a reduction in drag and, correspondingly, an increase in speed.

AIRCRAFT CONTROLS

Controlling an aircraft in flight involves a dazzling array of instruments and a large assortment of control devices. All of this instrumentation fills an area of the aircraft called the *cockpit* (Figs. 1-6, 1-7). The central control found in the cockpit is the *control yoke*. Various names have been applied to the control yoke, including *joystick, steering wheel*, and *controller*. No matter which name it uses, the control yoke serves as a direct physical connection between the pilot

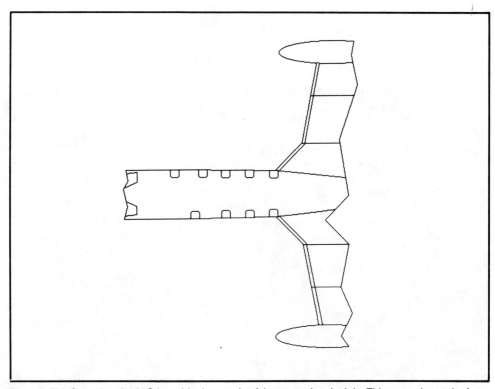

Fig. 1-5. The Gates Learjet 25G is an ideal example of the area rule principle. This narrowing at the fuselage/wing juncture reduces the drag caused by supersonic flight.

and the ailerons and the elevators. Additionally, two foot pedals give the pilot control over the movement of the aircraft's rudder. Therefore, all three axes of movement can be manipulated by the pilot by using the control yoke and the rudder pedals.

Pulling the control yoke back or pushing it forward moves the elevators up and down, respectively. The movement of the elevators, in turn, causes the aircraft to pitch up and down, respectively (Fig. 1-8). The final effect of this movement is that the aircraft will either climb or dive.

Moving the control yoke from side to side raises the aileron of one wing while lowering the aileron of the other wing. This movement rolls the aircraft in the direction of the raised aileron (Fig. 1-9). In other words, when the control yoke is moved to the left, the left wing aileron is raised and the right wing aileron is lowered. Similarly, when the control yoke is moved to the right, the left wing aileron is lowered and the right wing aileron is raised. The effect of this aileron movement is that in the first case the aircraft will roll to the left and in the second example the aircraft rolls to the right.

The final control device is the pair of rudder pedals that are located on the cockpit's floor. Only one rudder pedal is pushed at a time with the pilot's foot. This pushing causes the aircraft to rotate about the yaw axis (Fig. 1-10). As an example, when the pilot pushes the left rudder pedal, the rudder moves to the left. This makes the aircraft's nose yaw to the left. Likewise, when the pilot pushes the right rudder pedal, the rudder moves to the right. This rightward rudder movement causes the aircraft's nose to yaw to the right. Interestingly enough, the rudder pedals serve two different functions when the aircraft is on the ground.

Once an aircraft is on the ground, the vast majority of its airspeed has been eliminated. This loss in air movement reduces the effectiveness of the aircraft's control surfaces for directing the

9

Fig. 1-6. Inside the cockpit of a Cessna 182P Skylane. Dual controls are available for operating the aircraft's axes of movement. (courtesy Cessna Aircraft Company)

movement of the aircraft. In order to compensate for this loss of function, the rudder pedals take on a new role when the aircraft taxis about the ground. The rudder pedals are now used for moving either the nosewheel or tailwheel (the exact wheel location is dependent on the landing gear configuration). By using the rudder pedals in this fashion, an aircraft's ground movement becomes just a matter of steering.

Another ground function of the rudder pedals is the operation of the brakes. These brakes are located in the main wheels of the landing gear. By pushing both of the rudder pedals simultaneously, the wheel brakes are engaged and any rolling movement of the aircraft is stopped.

During flight, maintaining a true, level aircraft attitude can require that the pilot hold continual adjustments on the control surfaces. In the course of a prolonged flight, the constant application of this control can fatigue the pilot. Therefore, small auxiliary control surfaces are found on the elevators, ailerons, and rudder. These smaller surfaces are called *trim tabs*. Trim tabs share the same control principles as the larger control surfaces. By setting these trim tabs, the flight of the aircraft can be balanced, thereby freeing the pilot from having to exert constant pressure on the control surfaces. Trimming an aircraft is not the same as using a flight computer or autopilot function. Trim tabs merely aid in the balancing of an aircraft's control surfaces while in level flight.

Using just the rudder or just the ailerons for turning an aircraft will result in some undesirable side effects. Skids and slips disrupt attempts at rudder-only and aileron-only banks. Therefore, coordinated control surface applications are used during all formal turns and banks. A coordinated turn or bank combines both rudder and aileron movement. In a right bank, for example, both right rudder and right aileron are applied at the same time (a touch of up elevator might also be necessary). The resulting turn will be smooth and devoid of any skids or slips. This is called a *coordinated turn*. There are times, however, when coordinated control movement is unwanted—aerobatics is a good example. Flight Simulator has the ability to fly with either coordinated banks or uncoordinated aerobatics. Chapter 13 provides several maneuvers that take complete advantage of these uncoordinated aerobatic capabilities.

COMPUTER CONTROLS

Flight Simulator uses 44 to 66 different control commands (the difference is dependent on the

Fig. 1-7. A greater degree of sophistication is present in the layout of the Gates Learjet 25G cockpit. Not only are dual flight controls present, but many of the instruments are duplicated for both the pilot and the copilot. (courtesy Gates Learjet Corp.)

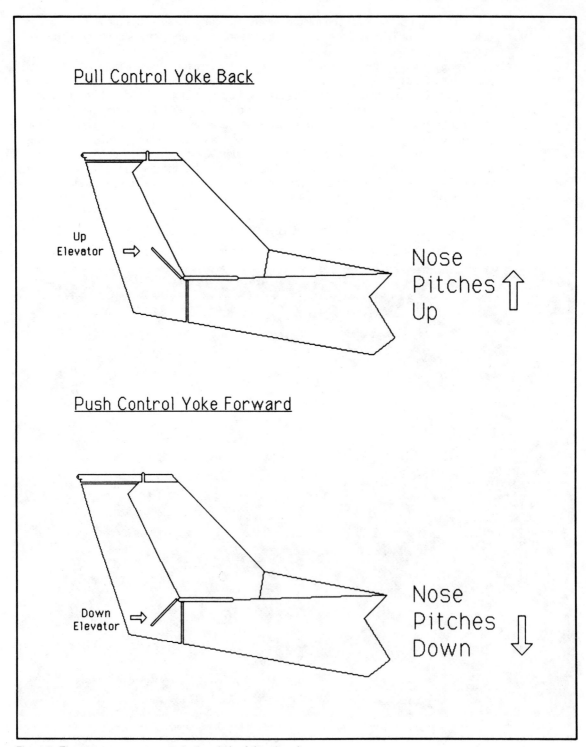

Fig. 1-8. Elevator movement controls the pitch of the aircraft.

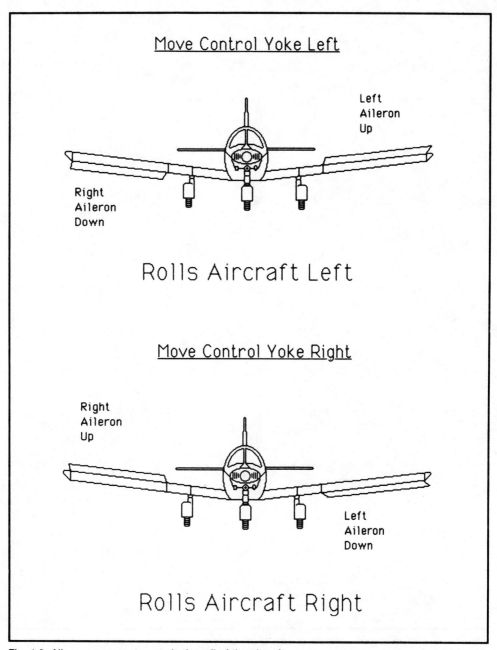

Fig. 1-9. Aileron movement controls the roll of the aircraft.

type of computer). All of these commands are operated through keyboard keystrokes and mouse movements. Alternatively, an optional joystick can be used for the manipulation of the aircraft's control surfaces in several of the different computer models. All of the possible keystrokes for each of the various computer models are listed in seven computer-specific tables. Table 1-1 lists all of the Flight Simulator commands for the Amiga computer. The Apple II family of computers'

13

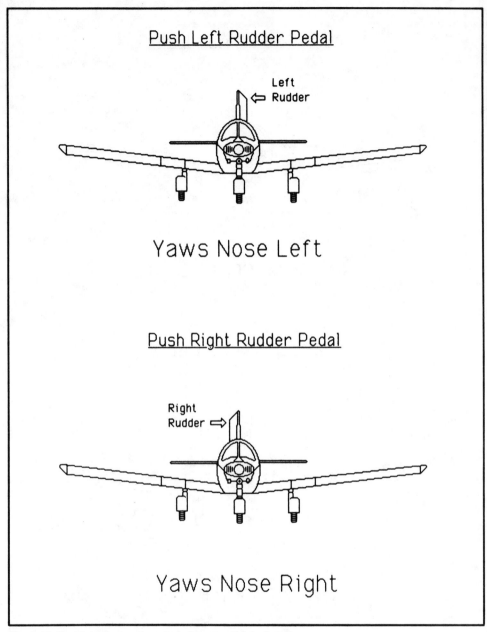

Fig. 1-10. Rudder movement controls the yaw of the aircraft.

commands, on the other hand, are listed in Table 1-2. Following in a similar mold, Atari 400, 600, 800, and 1200, Atari 520ST, Commodore 64/128, IBM PC family of computers, and Macintosh keyboard commands are provided in Tables 1-3 through 1-7, respectively. The terminology that is used for identifying each Flight Simulator control in each of these tables will be used throughout the remainder of this book. This universal language makes the instruction that is presented in the latter chapters much clearer and easier to understand. For example, the command

14

Table 1-1. Flight Simulator Keyboard Commands for the Amiga.

Command	Keystroke
Autopilot Off	Z
Autopilot On	Z
Backward View	B
Bank Left	4 + 0 (Keypad)
Bank Right	6 + . (Keypad)
Carburetor Heat	I
Control Tower Viewpoint Mode	C
Declare War	Shift + W
Downward View	G
Drop Bomb	Shift + X
Exit *Flight Simulator*	A
Fire Gun	Space
Flaps Extend	]
Flaps Retract	[
Forward View	T
Help	Help
Landing Gear Extend	U
Landing Gear Retract	U
Left View	F
Lights Off	L
Lights On	L
Magneto Adjust Left	1
Magneto Adjust Right	2
Magnification 1X	Backspace
Main 3D Window Off	F1
Main 3D Window On	F1
Map Display Off	F3
Map Display On	F3
Neutralize Bank	5 (Keypad)
Neutralize Pitch	5 (Keypad)
Neutralize Roll	5 (Keypad)
Nose Trim Down	)
Nose Trim Up	(
Pause	P
Pilot Viewpoint Mode	X
Pitch Nose Down	8 (Keypad)
Pitch Nose Up	2 (Keypad)
Right View	H
Roll Left	4 (Keypad)
Roll Right	6 (Keypad)
Save Current Flight Situation	Q
Secondary 3D Window Off	F2
Secondary 3D Window On	F2
Sound Off	Tab
Sound On	Tab
Spot Viewpoint Mode	S
Throttle Decrease	3 (Keypad)
Throttle Increase	9 (Keypad)
Track Viewpoint Mode	D
View Adjust	Cursor Keys
View Magnification Decrease	-
View Magnification Increase	+
View Magnification 1X	Backspace
War Report	Shift + E
Yaw Left	< or 0 (Keypad)
Yaw Right	> or . (Keypad)

Table 1-2. Flight Simulator Keyboard Commands for Apple II Computers.

Command	Keystroke
ADF Adjust	Control + A + >
Altimeter Adjust	Control + B
Backward View	5 + B
Bank Left	F + C
Bank Right	H + M
Brakes	Space Bar
Carburetor Heat	Control + I
COM Radio	Control + C + >
Declare War	Shift + W
Downward View	5 + G
Drop Bomb	Shift + X
Enter Editor	Escape
Exit *Flight Simulator*	Shift + +
Fire Gun	Space
Flaps Extend	N
Flaps Retract	Y
Forward View	5 + T
Fuel Tank Left	Control + F + <
Fuel Tank Right	Control + F + >
Heading Indicator Adjust	Control + D
Left View	5 + F
Lights Off	Control + L
Lights On	Control + L
Load Scenery Disk	Control + E
Magneto Adjust Left	Control + M + 3
Magneto Adjust Right	Control + M + 2
Main 3D Window Off	4
Main 3D Window On	5
Mixture Full	Control M + <
Mixture Rich	Control M + >
NAV 1 Adjust	Control + N + 1
NAV 2 Adjust	Control + N + 2
Neutralize Bank	G
Neutralize Pitch	G
Neutralize Roll	G
Nose Trim Down	R
Nose Trim Up	V
Pause	P
Pitch Nose Down	T
Pitch Nose Up	B
Radar Display Off	5
Radar Display On	4
Radar Magnification Decrease	4 + <
Radar Magnification Increase	4 + >
Read Library Mode	Control + X
Right View	5 + H
Roll Left	F
Roll Right	H
Save Current Flight Situation	S
Throttle Decrease	Left Arrow
Throttle Increase	Right Arrow
Transponder Adjust	Control + T
VOR OBS 1 Adjust	Control + V + 1
VOR OBS 2 Adjust	Control + V + 2
War Report	Shift + E
Yaw Left	C
Yaw Right	M

Table 1-3. Flight Simulator Keyboard Commands
for the Atari 400, 800, 600XL, 800XL, and 1200XL Computers.

Command	Keystroke
ADF Adjust	Control + A + >
Altimeter Adjust	Control + B
Backward View	5 + B
Bank Left	F + C
Bank Right	H + M
Brakes	Space Bar
Carburetor Heat	Control + I
COM Radio	Control + C + >
Declare War	Shift + W
Downward View	5 + G
Drop Bomb	Shift + X
Enter Editor	Escape
Exit *Flight Simulator*	Control + =
Fire Gun	Space
Flaps Extend	N
Flaps Retract	Y
Forward View	5 + T
Fuel Tank Left	Control + F + <
Fuel Tank Right	Control + F + >
Heading Indicator Adjust	Control + D
Left View	5 + F
Lights Off	Control + L
Lights On	Control + L
Load Scenery Disk	Control + E
Magneto Adjust Left	Control + M + 3
Magneto Adjust Right	Control + M + 2
Main 3D Window Off	4
Main 3D Window On	5
Mixture Full	Control M + <
Mixture Rich	Control M + >
NAV 1 Adjust	Control + N + 1
NAV 2 Adjust	Control + N + 2
Neutralize Bank	G
Neutralize Pitch	G
Neutralize Roll	G
Nose Trim Down	R
Nose Trim Up	V
Pause	P
Pitch Nose Down	T
Pitch Nose Up	B
Radar Display Off	5
Radar Display On	4
Radar Magnification Decrease	4 + <
Radar Magnification Increase	4 + >
Read Library Mode	Control + X
Right View	5 + H
Roll Left	F
Roll Right	H
Save Current Flight Situation	Control + S
Throttle Decrease	Left Arrow
Throttle Increase	Right Arrow
Transponder Adjust	Control + T
VOR OBS 1 Adjust	Control + V + 1
VOR OBS 2 Adjust	Control + V + 2
War Report	Shift + E
Yaw Left	C
Yaw Right	M

Table 1-4. Flight Simulator Keyboard Commands for the Atari 520ST.

Command	Keystroke
Autopilot Off	Z
Autopilot On	Z
Backward View	B
Bank Left	4 + 0 (Keypad)
Bank Right	6 + . (Keypad)
Carburetor Heat	I
Control Tower Viewpoint Mode	C
Declare War	Shift + W
Downward View	G
Drop Bomb	Shift + X
Exit *Flight Simulator*	A
Fire Gun	Space
Flaps Extend	]
Flaps Retract	[
Forward View	T
Help	Help
Landing Gear Extend	U
Landing Gear Retract	U
Left View	F
Lights Off	L
Lights On	L
Magneto Adjust Left	1
Magneto Adjust Right	2
Magnification 1X	Backspace
Main 3D Window Off	F1
Main 3D Window On	F1
Map Display Off	F3
Map Display On	F3
Neutralize Bank	5 (Keypad)
Neutralize Pitch	5 (Keypad)
Neutralize Roll	5 (Keypad)
Nose Trim Down	)
Nose Trim Up	(
Pause	P
Pilot Viewpoint Mode	X
Pitch Nose Down	8 (Keypad)
Pitch Nose Up	2 (Keypad)
Right View	H
Roll Left	4 (Keypad)
Roll Right	6 (Keypad)
Save Current Flight Situation	Q
Secondary 3D Window Off	F2
Secondary 3D Window On	F2
Sound Off	Tab
Sound On	Tab
Spot Viewpoint Mode	S
Throttle Decrease	3 (Keypad)
Throttle Increase	9 (Keypad)
Track Viewpoint Mode	D
View Adjust	Cursor Keys
View Magnification Decrease	-
View Magnification Increase	+
View Magnification 1X	Backspace
War Report	Shift + E
Yaw Left	< or 0 (Keypad)
Yaw Right	> or . (Keypad)

**Table 1-5. Flight Simulator Keyboard Commands
for the Commodore 64 and Commodore 128 Computers.**

Command	Keystroke
ADF Adjust	Control + A + >
Altimeter Adjust	Control + B
Backward View	5 + B
Bank Left	F + C
Bank Right	H + M
Brakes	Space Bar
Carburetor Heat	Control + I
COM Radio	Control + C + >
Declare War	Shift + W
Downward View	5 + G
Drop Bomb	Shift + X
Enter Editor	E
Exit *Flight Simulator*	+
Fire Gun	Space
Flaps Extend	N
Flaps Retract	Y
Forward View	5 + T
Fuel Tank Left	Control + F + <
Fuel Tank Right	Control + F + >
Heading Indicator Adjust	Control + D
Left View	5 + F
Lights Off	Control + L
Lights On	Control + L
Load Scenery Disk	Control + E
Magneto Adjust Left	Control + M + 3
Magneto Adjust Right	Control + M + 2
Main 3D Window Off	4
Main 3D Window On	5
Mixture Full	Control M + <
Mixture Rich	Control M + >
NAV 1 Adjust	Control + N + 1
NAV 2 Adjust	Control + N + 2
Neutralize Bank	G
Neutralize Pitch	G
Neutralize Roll	G
Nose Trim Down	R
Nose Trim Up	V
Pause	P
Pitch Nose Down	T
Pitch Nose Up	B
Radar Display Off	5
Radar Display On	4
Radar Magnification Decrease	4 + <
Radar Magnification Increase	4 + >
Read Library Mode	Control + X
Right View	5 + H
Roll Left	F
Roll Right	H
Save Current Flight Situation	S
Throttle Decrease	[
Throttle Increase	]
Transponder Adjust	Control + T
VOR OBS 1 Adjust	Control + V + 1
VOR OBS 2 Adjust	Control + V + 2
War Report	Shift + E
Yaw Left	C
Yaw Right	M

Table 1-6. Flight Simulator Keyboard Commands for IBM PC Computers.

Command	Keystroke
Altimeter Adjust	A
Backward View	Scroll Lock + B
Bank Left	4 + 0 (Keypad)
Bank Right	6 + + (Keypad)
Brakes	.
Carburetor Heat	H
COM Radio	C
Declare War	Shift + W
Downward View	Scroll Lock + G
Drop Bomb	Shift + X
Enter Editor	Escape
Fire Gun	Space
Flaps Extend	F3, F5, F7, F9
Flaps Retract	F1
Forward View	Sroll Lock + T
Heading Indicator Adjust	D
Left View	Scroll Lock + F
Lights Off	L
Lights On	L
Load Scenery Disk	Control + E
Magneto Adjust Left	M
Magneto Adjust Right	M
Main 3D Window Off	Num Lock
Main 3D Window On	Scroll Lock
Mixture Full	M
Mixture Rich	M
NAV 1 Adjust	N
NAV 2 Adjust	N
Neutralize Bank	5 (Keypad)
Neutralize Pitch	5 (Keypad)
Neutralize Roll	5 (Keypad)
Nose Trim Down	7 (Keypad)
Nose Trim Up	1 (Keypad)
Pause	P
Pitch Nose Down	8 (Keypad)
Pitch Nose Up	2 (Keypad)
Radar Display Off	Scroll Lock
Radar Display On	Num Lock
Radar Magnification Decrease	-
Radar Magnification Increase	+
Read Library Mode	Escape + L
Right View	Scroll Lock + H
Roll Left	4 (Keypad)
Roll Right	6 (Keypad)
Save Current Flight Situation	Escape + S
Throttle Decrease	F8
Throttle Increase	F4
Transponder Adjust	T
VOR OBS 1 Adjust	V
VOR OBS 2 Adjust	V
War Report	Shift + E
Yaw Left	0 (Keypad)
Yaw Right	+ (Keypad)

Table 1-7. Flight Simulator Keyboard Commands for the Macintosh.

Command	Keystroke
Autopilot Off	Z
Autopilot On	Z
Backward View	B
Carburetor Heat	I
Control Tower Viewpoint Mode	C
Declare War	Shift + W
Downward View	G
Drop Bomb	Shift + X
Exit *Flight Simulator*	A
Fire Gun	Space
Flaps Extend	]
Flaps Retract	[
Forward View	T
Landing Gear Extend	U
Landing Gear Retract	U
Left View	F
Lights Off	L
Lights On	L
Magneto Adjust Left	1
Magneto Adjust Right	2
Magnification 1X	Backspace
Map Display Off	M
Map Display On	M
Nose Trim Down	0
Nose Trim Up	9
Pause	P
Pilot Viewpoint Mode	X
Right View	H
Save Current Flight Situation	Q
Secondary 3D Window Off	Option
Secondary 3D Window On	Option
Sound Off	'
Sound On	'
Spot Viewpoint Mode	S
Track Viewpoint Mode	D
View Magnification Decrease	-
View Magnification Increase	+
View Magnification 1X	Backspace
War Report	Shift + E
Yaw Left	,
Yaw Right	.

"adjust the magnetos," is interpreted as meaning:

☐ Press the Ctrl + M key combination for the Apple *IIe*.
☐ Press the 1 and 2 keys or click the Magnetos Indicator in cursor mode for the Macintosh.
☐ Press the M key for the IBM PC.
☐ As an instructional aid, you may wish to make a copy of the required table and place it next to your keyboard during flight.

HARDWARE SYSTEM REQUIREMENTS

The actual computer hardware required for flying Flight Simulator varies according to each particular computer brand. Along with these different hardware requirements are an equally different set of startup instructions.

Amiga. The keyboard and the mouse serve as the primary user interface. All three of the aircraft's axes of movement are manipulated through selective mouse movements. Additionally, the mouse also serves as a throttle and brake control.

A unique feature of the Amiga version of Flight Simulator is the ability for multi-player flight. In this mode of operation, two different pilots can fly aircraft during the same flight. Basically, this form of flight is achieved through a direct communication link between two different computers (either another Amiga or an Atari 520ST) via a serial cable. Once both computers have been properly connected, they are both placed in the multi-player mode found exclusively on the Amiga and Atari 520ST versions of Flight Simulator. An exciting attribute of this flight mode is that the two pilots can be either in the same room or they can communicate with each other over a modem/telephone line connection.

Starting Flight Simulator on an Amiga is a simple three-step procedure:

☐ Turn on the Amiga.
☐ Place the Flight Simulator floppy disk in the Amiga's internal disk drive.
☐ The program will load automatically.

The program will now load into the computer's memory. After several seconds, your Cessna 182 is idling on runway 27 Right at the Oakland International Airport. In order to select various setup parameters, the File Menu on the Menu Bar is pulled down with the mouse. A specific setup mode is chosen by highlighting the desired menu selection.

For a demonstration flight:
Highlight Demo.
For a demonstration flight without any sound effects:
Highlight Quiet Demo.
For the normal piston-powered flight mode:
Highlight Prop.
For the normal Gates Learjet flight mode:
Highlight Jet.
For the simulated combat mode:
Highlight WWI Ace.
To exit Flight Simulator:
Highlight Quit.

Your Amiga is now ready for flight.

Apple. Virtually any "standard" Apple II computer is able to run Flight Simulator. This all-inclusive blanket statement represents the following Apple computer models: Apple II, Apple II +, Apple IIe, and Apple IIc. Apple-compatible computers, such as the Franklins, Laser 128, and Apple IIGS, should also run Flight Simulator, although the veracity of this speculation has not been proven.

Besides the Apple II computer, you will also need a floppy disk drive and a monitor for flying Flight Simulator. An optional joystick can be added to this arrangement for controlling the aircraft's three axes of movement.

The joystick that can be added to the flight system is of questionable value, however. Due to the large number of keyboard-based instrument controls, joystick flight can be impractical. Moving your hands back and forth between the keyboard and the joystick frustrates the smooth operation of the aircraft. In light of all of these negative aspects, a joystick does lend an air of realism to the flight simulator. Therefore, if you demand this level of realistic flight, plug the joystick into the Apple's joystick port.

After you have assembled all of the required hardware, it is time to start the program. Only two steps are necessary for beginning Flight Simulator:

☐ Place the Flight Simulator floppy disk in disk drive 1 of your Apple computer system.
☐ Turn on the computer. (This method is the auto-boot starting technique.)
☐ Alternatively, if your computer is already on, insert the Flight Simulator disk into disk drive 1 and press the Control + Open Apple + Reset key combination.

When the program has been loaded, you are presented with a menu for selecting the type of monitor that you are using.

An Apple system with a color monitor:
Press A.
An Apple system with a monochrome monitor:
Press B.

The final Apple setup procedure is the operating mode menu selection:

For a demonstration flight:
Press A.
For the normal flight mode (this is the mode that is used throughout this book):
Press B.

Your Apple system is now ready for flight.

Atari. Atari 400, 800, 600XL, 800XL, and 1200XL computer owners will need very little "extra" equipment in order to fly Flight Simulator. In addition to the Atari, only a floppy disk drive and a monitor are necessary for completing your piston-powered flight simulator. You may also add an optional joystick for moving the aircraft's three axes control surfaces.

Setting up your flight simulator is remarkably easy. Just plug the floppy disk drive into the computer's disk drive port. This step should be performed with the power to the computer system switched off.

Next, attach your monitor to the computer's RF (Radio Frequency) output socket. If you are using a television set (either color or black and white) as your monitor, then you might need to attach a TV switch box between the Atari's RF plug and the TV's antenna leads. Some of the more recent models of television sets incorporate a special game plug into their design, thereby eliminating the need for this box. If, on the other hand, you are using a color composite monitor, a different Atari socket will provide the output. In this case, a special composite video socket produces the video and audio signals for this type of monitor.

Finally, a joystick can be added to your flight system. This is an unnecessary item that is best avoided. Basically, the large number of keyboard-based instrument controls makes joystick flight impractical. Switching one's hands back and forth between the joystick and keyboard is an unwanted distraction in an already congested environment. If you feel that the realism of joystick control surface operation is vital to your enjoyment of Flight Simulator, then plug one joystick into the Atari's joystick port.

Starting Flight Simulator on the Atari is a simple three-step procedure:

☐ Turn on your Atari system disk drive.
☐ Place the Flight Simulator floppy disk in the disk drive and close the door.
☐ Turn on the Atari computer.

Once the program has been loaded, you are presented with a menu for determining the type of monitor that you are using.

An Atari system with a color monitor:
Press A.
An Atari system with a black and white monitor:
Press B.
    Concluding the Atari setup procedure is the operating mode selection menu:
For a demonstration flight:
Press A.
For the normal flight mode (this is the mode that is used throughout this book):
Press B.

    Your Atari system is now ready for flight.
    Atari 520ST. The keyboard and the mouse serve as the primary user interface. All three of the aircraft's axes of movement are manipulated through selective mouse movements. Additionally, the mouse also serves as a throttle and brake control.
    Like the Amiga, a unique feature of the Atari 520ST version of Flight Simulator is the ability for multi-player flight. In this mode of operation, two different pilots can fly aircraft during the same flight. Basically, this form of flight is achieved through a direct communication link between two different computers (either another Atari 520ST or an Amiga) via a serial cable. Once both of the computers have been properly connected, they are both placed in the multi-player mode found exclusively on the Amiga and Atari 520ST versions of Flight Simulator. An exciting attribute of this flight mode is that the two pilots can be either in the same room or they can communicate with each other over a modem/telephone line connection.
    Starting Flight Simulator on an Atari 520ST is a simple three-step procedure:

    ☐ Turn on the Atari 520ST.
    ☐ Place the Flight Simulator floppy disk in the Atari's external disk drive.
    ☐ The program will load automatically.

    The program will now load into the computer's memory. After several seconds, your Cessna 182 is idling on runway 27 Right at the Oakland International Airport. In order to select various setup parameters, the File Menu on the Menu Bar is pulled down with the mouse. A specific setup mode is chosen by highlighting the desired menu selection.

For a demonstration flight:
Highlight Demo.
For a demonstration flight without any sound effects:
Highlight Quiet Demo.
For the normal piston-powered flight mode:
Highlight Prop.
For the normal Gates Learjet flight mode:
Highlight Jet.
For the simulated combat mode:
Highlight WWI Ace.
To exit Flight Simulator:
Highlight Quit.

    Your Atari 520ST is now ready for flight.
    Commodore. Commodore 64/128 computer owners will need very little ''extra'' equipment

in order to fly Flight Simulator. In addition to the C-64 or C-128, only a floppy disk drive and a monitor are necessary for completing your piston-powered flight simulator. You may also add an optional joystick for moving the aircraft's three-axis control surfaces.

Setting up your flight simulator is remarkably easy. The floppy disk drive can be either the older single-sided Commodore 1541 or the newer double-sided Commodore 1571. Whichever model is used, connect it to the computer's serial plug.

Next, attach your monitor to the computer's RF (Radio Frequency) output socket. If you are using a television set (either color or black and white) as your monitor, then you might need to attach a TV switch box between the Commodore's RF plug and the TV's antenna leads. Some of the more recent models of television sets incorporate a special game plug into their design, thereby eliminating the need for this box. If, on the other hand, you are using a color composite monitor, a different Commodore socket will provide the output. In this case, a special composite video socket produces the video and audio signals for this type of monitor.

Finally, a joystick can be added to your flight system. This is an unnecessary item that is best avoided. Basically, the large number of keyboard-based instrument controls makes joystick flight impractical. Switching one's hands back and forth between the joystick and keyboard is an unwanted distraction in an already congested environment. If you feel that the realism of joystick control surface operation is vital to your enjoyment of Flight Simulator, then plug one joystick into the Commodore's control port 1.

Starting Flight Simulator on the Commodore 64/128 is a simple three-step procedure:

☐ Turn on your Commodore system. (Commodore 128 owners will need to enter the C-64 mode before performing the next step. To do this, type GO64 at the READY prompt.)
☐ Place the Flight Simulator floppy disk in the disk drive and close the door.
☐ Type the following command:

LOAD ''*'',8,1

and press the Return key.

Once the program has been loaded, you are presented with a menu for determining the type of monitor that you are using.

A Commodore system with a color monitor:
Press A.
A Commodore system with a black and white monitor:
Press B.

Concluding the Commodore setup procedure is the operating mode selection menu:
For a demonstration flight:
Press A.
For the normal flight mode (this is the mode that is used throughout this book):
Press B.

Your Commodore system is now ready for flight.

IBM. An enormous variety of different hardware products can be used with complete success on the IBM PC computer. This includes the IBM PC, PC XT, PC AT, and PCjr models. Essentially, these IBM computers must have a minimum of 128K bytes of RAM (random access memory), a graphics card, and a monitor. A joystick can be used optionally for control over the aircraft's three axes of movement.

One question that is bound to pop up concerns the use of Flight Simulator with IBM PC-compatible computers. Theoretically, every computer that sports a high degree of compatibility should run Flight Simulator without any problems. As to actual tests, three different brands have been evaluated: Compaq, Heath/Zenith, and Tandy. All three of these manufacturers' products flew Flight Simulator without fault. This statement isn't intended to serve as an endorsement, but rather a yardstick for you to use in your own compatibility tests.

The minimal memory requirement of 128K bytes of RAM shouldn't pose a problem to any of the IBM models (and other compatibles, for that matter). There is a degree of dissatisfaction, however, among IBM PC computer owners who have hard disk drives in their systems. This dissent arises from the Flight Simulator copy protection scheme. Many of these users wish that they could install Flight Simulator on their hard disk drives. Unfortunately, subLOGIC neglected to allow for such a provision. If hard disk drive installation is a desire of yours, there is a special program available from TranSec Systems, Inc. (1802-200 North University Drive, Plantation, FL 33322 (305) 474-7548; ask for Twin-Pak #201) that removes the copy protection from Flight Simulator (and its associated Scenery Disks). The result is a non-copy-protected disk that can be installed on any hard disk drive or RAM disk drive.

There are three basic types of graphics cards that can be used with Flight Simulator: the IBM Color/Graphics Monitor Adapter, the Hercules Graphics Card, and the IBM Enhanced Graphics and Adapter. Of course, there is a vast assortment of cards and adapters that match the standards established by these three products. For example, the Paradise Modular Graphics Card, the AST Preview!, and the Tecmar EGA Master all duplicate the respective features of the three Flight Simulator standards. Once again, only these three graphics card substitutes have been actually tested for Flight Simulator compatibility. Other brands and models might not provide a sufficient degree of compatibility.

After the proper graphics card has been installed, only a monitor is required to complete the flight simulation system. In order to obtain the highest amount of image resolution, the IBM Monochrome Display, IBM Color Display, or the IBM Enhanced Color Display should be used with the appropriate graphics card (this includes all comparable monitors). Composite monitors and TV sets, while they will work, should be avoided due to their lower screen resolution.

One final item that can be added to your Flight Simulator flight system is a joystick. This is an unnecessary option that should be avoided. Basically, the large number of keyboard-based instrument controls makes joystick flight impractical. Switching one's hands back and forth between the joystick and keyboard is an unwanted distraction in an already congested environment. Conversely, a quality joystick such as CH Products' Mach III could actually improve your Flight Simulator performance. If you feel that the realism of joystick control surface operation is vital to your enjoyment of Flight Simulator, then plug one joystick into an IBM game port (on the IBM PCjr use the joystick 1 port). A special game port interface card must be used for the connection of the joystick. The Quadram Expanded Quadboard is an example of a card that has a game port interface.

Starting Flight Simulator on an IBM PC computer is a simple two-step procedure:

☐ Place the Flight Simulator floppy disk in disk drive A and close the door.
☐ Turn on your IBM PC computer. (Flight Simulator can also be booted from a previously started IBM PC by simultaneously pressing the Ctrl + Alt + Del key combination.)

There are several optional methods for starting Flight Simulator which implement all of the different graphics card options.

☐ Load PC-DOS. Place the Flight Simulator floppy disk in disk drive A and close the door.
For a Hercules Graphics Card system:
☐ From the DOS prompt, type:
A>FS H

and press the Enter Key.
For an IBM EGA monochrome system:
   □ From the DOS prompt, type:
   A > FS M
and press the Enter key.
For an IBM EGA color system:
   □ From the DOS prompt, type:
   A > FS E
and press the Enter key.
For non-copy-protected hard disk drive systems:
   □ From the DOS prompt, type:
   C > FS
and press the Enter key.
(Hard disk drive users can also use one of the other graphics card/monitor starting commands.)

   Once the program has been loaded, you are presented with three menus for determining
the type of monitor that you are using, the nature of the computer's keyboard, and the program's
operating mode.

The monitor menu—
An IBM PC system with a composite monitor or a color TV:
Press A.
An IBM PC system with a black and white TV or monitor:
Press B.
An IBM PC system with an RGB monitor:
Press C.
The operating mode menu—
For a demonstration flight:
Press A.
For the normal flight mode (this is the mode that is used throughout this book):
Press B.
To make a single backup copy of the Flight Simulator floppy disk:
Press C.
For a demonstration flight without any sound effects:
Press D.
The keyboard menu—
An IBM PCjr system:
Press A.
An IBM PC (e.g., PC, PC XT, and PC AT) system:
Press B.

   Your IBM system is now ready for flight.
   Macintosh. Flying Flight Simulator on the Macintosh follows the same setup procedure as
has been previously described for the Amiga and Atari 520ST computers. Once again, the keyboard and the mouse serve as the primary user interface. One minor difference between the
Macintosh implementation of Flight Simulator versus the Amiga and Atari 520ST versions is found
in the single-button Macintosh mouse. Even though the same control functions have been assigned to this Cyclopean mouse, a slightly different access technique is used for duplicating the
two-button mouse's abilities. Double-clicking and dragging are the two principal means for making the uni-button Mac mouse resemble the Amiga and Atari 520ST bi-button versions.

The prosperity of the Apple Computer Macintosh line has ushered in an interesting problem for software vendors. Currently there are four different Macintosh models with several others pending release. Each of these Macintosh varieties sports refinements in its RAM, ROM, mass storage capabilities, and I/O (Input/Output) ports. In reference to Flight Simulator, only one of these Macintosh features deserves closer inspection. The amount of RAM that is available to the Macintosh determines the complexity of flight. For example, any Macintosh with less than 512K bytes of RAM (this includes the original 128K Macintosh) will be unable to use all of the Flight Simulator controls and instrumentation. A further limitation of the 128K Mac is that none of the scenarios presented in Sections II, VI, and VII can be simulated with this computer. Therefore, 128K Mac owners will be limited in their ability to duplicate all of the historical aviation scenarios that are presented in this book.

One piece of optional equipment that can make your Macintosh flight experience more exciting is an ImageWriter II printer. Unlike all of the other Flight Simulator computer versions, the Macintosh version is able to make high-resolution screen dumps of actual in-flight events. This feature will allow you to preserve those special aerial moments when you successfully complete one of the 82 historical scenarios. In addition to the standard Macintosh Shift + Command + 4 screen dump keystroke, a unique poster printing capability has been added to the Flight Simulator software. For example, pressing a Command + 5 keystroke combination saves the current flight screen on a floppy disk in an enlarged 12 page format. This floppy disk must have at least 200K bytes of free space for holding this screen save. During this screen save process, 12 different MacPaint files are created on the floppy disk. Pressing a Command + 6 keystroke combination prints the current flight screen directly on an attached ImageWriter II printer. This screen dump will take 12 sheets of paper for printing the enlarged screen image.

The final result from either one of these special poster production procedures is a large 24 × 18 inch mural. But the fun doesn't have to stop here. Hand-coloring this final poster can transform the anachronistic black/white printout into a handsome contemporary wall covering. Or a small, three-dimensional cockpit can be created with cutout instrument dials from one of these posters. If nothing else, these extracurricular activities will supplement your fundamental knowledge of flight.

Starting Flight Simulator on a Macintosh is a simple three-step procedure:

☐ Turn on the Macintosh. (Alternatively, if your Macintosh is already on, press the programmer's reset button on the left side of the computer.)
☐ Place the Flight Simulator floppy disk in the Macintosh's internal disk drive.
☐ The desktop will appear. Double-click on the Flight Simulator icon.

The program will now load into the computer's memory. After several seconds, your Cessna 182 is idling on runway 27 Right at the Oakland International Airport. In order to select various setup parameters, the File Menu on the Menu Bar is pulled down with the mouse. A specific setup mode is chosen by highlighting the desired menu selection.

For a demonstration flight:
Highlight Demo.
For a demonstration flight without any sound effects:
Highlight Quiet Demo.
For the normal piston-powered flight mode:
Highlight Prop.
For the normal Gates Learjet flight mode:
Highlight Jet.
For the simulated combat mode:
Highlight WWI Ace.

To exit Flight Simulator and eject the floppy disk:
Highlight Quit.

Your Macintosh is now ready for flight.

THE COMPUTER COCKPIT

No matter which computer version of Flight Simulator you are flying, the operation of the controls and the representation of the instruments remains the same.

The Instrument Panel. All of the aircraft's instrumentation and current flight status are displayed on the computer system's monitor. The format of the monitor's screen closely approximates the amount of information that is contained on a contemporary aircraft's instrument panel. Figure 1-11 shows the instrument panel on an Apple Computer Macintosh computer system. Refer to your respective computer's instruction manual during the following explanation of the Flight Simulator controls and instruments.

AIRSPEED INDICATOR—gives the true airspeed of the aircraft in knots.

ARTIFICIAL HORIZON—displays the aircraft's pitch and bank attitudes relative to the earth's horizon. This instrument is also known as the *Attitude Indicator*.

ALTIMETER—shows the aircraft's altitude in feet above sea level.

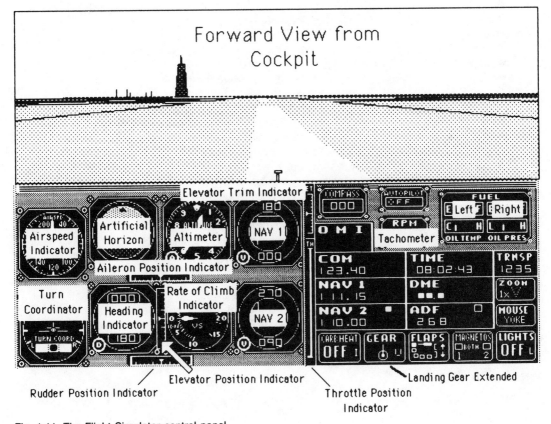

Fig. 1-11. The Flight Simulator control panel.

TURN COORDINATOR—indicates the turn rate and the amount of coordination during a bank.

HEADING INDICATOR—the aircraft's current direction is displayed as a magnetic heading in compass degrees.

RATE OF CLIMB INDICATOR—measures the speed of either a climb or a descent.

COMPASS—a typical magnetic compass.

OMNI-BEARING INDICATOR (OBI)—a navigational instrument also used during landing approaches for tuning VOR radio beacons. There are two OBIs, one for each NAV radio.

CLOCK—a typical digital clock.

OUTER, MIDDLE, AND INNER MARKER LIGHTS (OMI)—a landing instrument which indicates where the aircraft is situated over the runway marker beacons.

FUEL QUANTITY INDICATORS—a gauge for each of the aircraft's internal wing fuel tanks.

OIL TEMPERATURE GAUGE—indicates the temperature of the aircraft engine's oil.

OIL PRESSURE GAUGE—indicates the engine's oil pressure.

TACHOMETER—a digital scale of the engine's true rpm (revolutions per minute). (On the Gates Learjet, the tachometer indicates the percentage of full rpm. In other words, a reading of 100 would mean full power or 100 percent rpm.)

NAV 1 RADIO—a 200-channel navigational radio that is used for tuning VOR and ILS frequencies.

NAV 2 RADIO—the same features as found on NAV 1 Radio. This second radio serves as both a backup and a system for double-checking the aircraft's current position.

DISTANCE MEASURING EQUIPMENT (DME)—a digital scale of the number of nautical miles from the tuned VOR.

AUTOMATIC DIRECTION FINDER (ADF)—a navigational instrument for determining the aircraft's relative bearing.

COM RADIO—a 360-channel transceiver that is tuned to the airport's ATIS.

TRANSPONDER—a radio that identifies the aircraft on ATC radar.

AILERON POSITION INDICATOR—shows the current position of the aircraft's ailerons.

ELEVATOR POSITION INDICATOR—shows the current position of the aircraft's elevators.

RUDDER POSITION INDICATOR—shows the current position of the aircraft's rudders. In coordinated flight, both the aileron and rudder position indicators move together.

THROTTLE POSITION INDICATOR—shows the current throttle setting.

ELEVATOR TRIM INDICATOR—shows the amount of elevator trim.

CARBURETOR HEAT INDICATOR—shows whether the carburetor heat is on or off.

LANDING GEAR STATUS INDICATOR—displays whether the landing gear is extended or retracted.

FLAP POSITION INDICATOR—indicates the current position of the aircraft's flaps.

MAGNETOS INDICATOR—displays whether the left or right (or both) magnetos are on or off. This indicator also displays the status of the carburetor mixture setting.

LIGHTS INDICATOR—shows whether the aircraft's interior and exterior lights are on or off.

Several of these instruments share a unique range of values.

AIRSPEED INDICATOR—0 to 200 knots.

ALTIMETER—0 to 20,000 feet.

HEADING INDICATOR—0 to 359 degrees, where 0 degrees is north and 180 degrees is south.

RATE OF CLIMB INDICATOR—0 to 2000 feet per minute. There are positive and negative values for this indicator depending on whether the aircraft is climbing or diving.

Instrument Selection. There is one instrument that can be alternately engaged and disengaged at the pilot's discretion.

RADAR—provides an overview of the area that is currently being flown in by the aircraft.

Operation: An active Radar shows all of the ground terrain. A small "plus" symbol is used to indicate your aircraft's current position. By zooming the scale in and out, the Radar's magnification can be altered to any given situation. For example, taxiing around an airport will require a greater degree of magnification than is needed for identifying a given landmark from the air.

Note: On the 68000 Flight Simulator versions, the Radar is referred to as the Map display. Its operation, however, is identical to that described for the Radar display.

Aircraft Controls. The actual flying of Flight Simulator is performed by six controls.

ELEVATOR—controls the pitch movement of the aircraft.

Operation: Neutralizing the controls will halt the aircraft's pitch rotation. The optional joystick operates this control.

AILERONS PLUS RUDDER—control the roll and bank movement of the aircraft.

Operation: A bank is produced by constantly holding either a left or right aileron plus rudder combination. Neutralizing the controls will halt the aircraft's roll and bank rotation. The optional joystick operates this control.

THROTTLE—increases or decreases the amount of rpm generated by the engine.

Operation: A sustained holding of either the increase or decrease throttle key will continuously raise or lower the amount of engine thrust.

LANDING GEAR—used for landing the aircraft and subsequent taxi control.

Visual Orientation. Good pilot visibility is the key to successful flight. There are four different viewpoint modes and five different view directions.

COCKPIT MODE—a view from the aircraft's cockpit.

TOWER MODE—a view from the control tower of the airport. (This mode is only available with the 68000 versions.)

TRACK MODE—a "moving" view from the control tower of the airport. In other words, the tower view moves along with your aircraft. (This mode is only available with the 68000 versions.)

SPOT MODE—a view from a nearby "spotter" aircraft which matches your speed and flight pattern. (This mode is only available with the 68000 versions.)

FORWARD VIEW—looking straight ahead, out the front of the canopy.

BACKWARD VIEW—looking over the pilot's shoulder, out the rear of the canopy.

DOWNWARD VIEW—looking straight down, out the bottom of the cockpit.

RIGHT VIEW—looking out the right side of the cockpit.

LEFT VIEW—looking out the left side of the cockpit.

In all of the viewpoint modes and view directions, the view magnification can be altered to suit the needs of a particular visual situation with the 68000 versions.

Miscellaneous Controls. There are seven remaining Flight Simulator controls that serve as system maintenance features.

AUTOPILOT—turns the aircraft's autopilot control on or off. (This feature is found only on the 68000 versions.)

EDITOR—enters the simulation parameter editor. (This feature is not found on the 68000 versions.)

PAUSE—stops all of the Flight Simulator action so that you can catch your breath or plot a strategy.

SAVE—saves the current flight simulation on a floppy disk.

SECOND WINDOW—opens another three-dimensional window in the cockpit. (This feature is found only on the 68000 versions.)

SOUND—turns the sound effects on or off. (This feature is found only on the 68000 versions.)

RESET FLIGHT SIMULATOR—stops the current flight simulation and returns to the initial program starting point. (This feature is found only on the 68000 versions.)

Chapter 2

Orientation Flight

The best way to become familiar with the function of the numerous aircraft controls is to take Flight Simulator up for a quick "hands-off" test flight. This initial flight will only cover a minimal amount of instructional material. Basically, you will just take off, level the aircraft at a shallow altitude, turn back toward the airport, and land. Remarkably, this entire flight is visually contained on the following pages. Therefore, Flight Simulator doesn't even need to be booted for this initial flight.

Another important facet of the flight instruction that is provided in this chapter deals with the manner of its presentation. This material shares the same format that will be used for conducting all of the historical aviation scenarios that are detailed in Part II of this book. Don't slough over the importance of learning this instructional method at this early stage. Only when you thoroughly understand this format will you then be able to concentrate on perfecting your flying technique.

CESSNA/PIPER ORIENTATION FLIGHT

Use the appropriate Flight Simulator starting method as discussed in Chapter 1. With the initial computer-oriented menu(s) correctly answered, begin the orientation flight setup.

   Flight Setup. The environmental and reality factors will use the default settings.

   Flight Objectives. Your goal during this flight is to successfully follow a 10-step orientation flight.

   Filing the Flight Plan. Figure 2-1 is an aerial view of Meigs Field in Chicago, Illinois. Your aircraft is sitting on runway 36. Your heading is 0 degrees (facing due north). The fuel reading is full and the throttle is at 650 rpm. The altimeter is set for an altitude of 592 feet. You have a forward view with a view magnification of 1 x.

   Step 1. From your holding position, increase throttle to 2200 rpm. Begin your takeoff roll (Fig. 2-2).

   Step 2. As your airspeed increases, slowly give a slight amount of up elevator. The aircraft will become airborne at approximately 60 knots (Fig. 2-3).

   Step 3. At an altitude of 1000 feet, reduce the throttle setting to 1750 rpm. Neutralize the

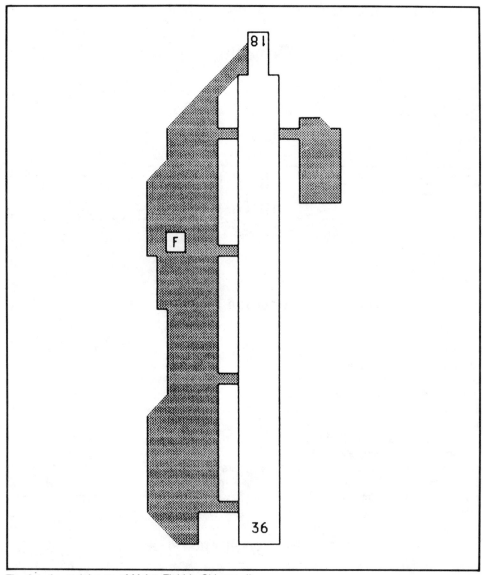

Fig. 2-1. An aerial map of Meigs Field in Chicago, IL.

elevator and level the aircraft. Retract the landing gear (Fig. 2-4).

Step 4. Switch the view direction to a Left View. Watch for the appearance of the John Hancock Building. Even with the elevator neutralized, the aircraft will continue to gain altitude (Fig. 2-5).

Step 5. When the John Hancock Building is directly off the port wing, execute a left bank. Neutralize the ailerons/rudder combination (Fig. 2-6).

Step 6. Assume a compass heading of 160 degrees. Meigs Field is visible out the Forward View. Watch your altitude. Don't let the aircraft rise above 3000 feet (Fig. 2-7).

Step 7. Switch to a Downward View. Look for the airport as you pass over its location (Fig. 2-8).

Step 8. Return to the Forward View. Begin your descent. Reduce the throttle to 1600 rpm and give a slight amount of down elevator. Remain on the heading of 160 degrees (Fig. 2-9).

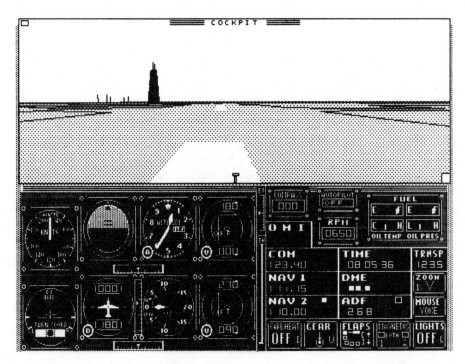

Fig. 2-2. Lined up ready for takeoff.

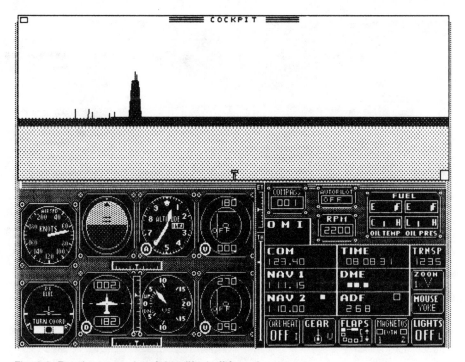

Fig. 2-3. Rotation; your aircraft has lifted off from the runway.

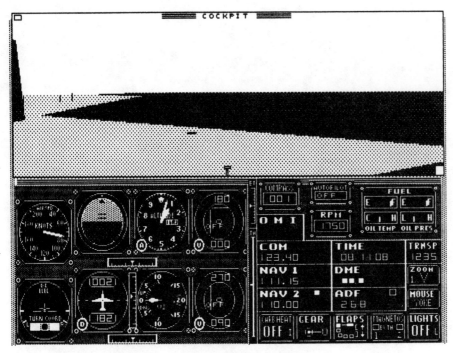

Fig. 2-4. The landing gear has been retracted and the engine is at cruising speed.

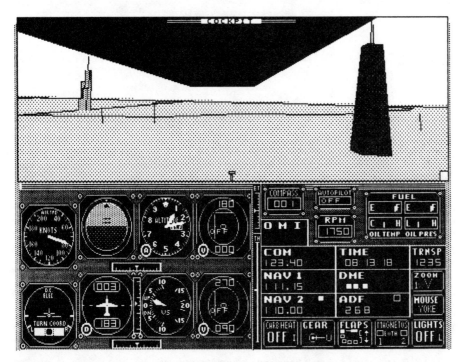

Fig. 2-5. Looking out the left cockpit window.

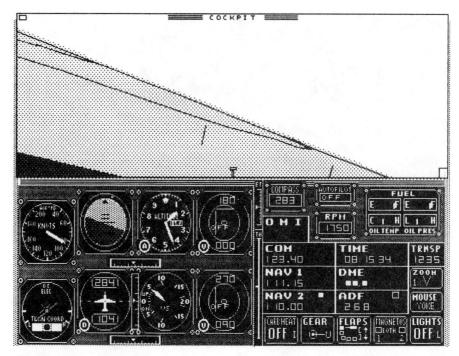

Fig. 2-6. Entering a left bank.

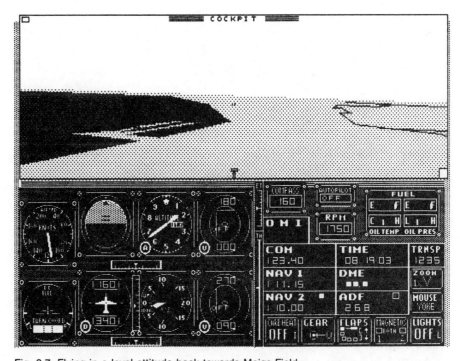

Fig. 2-7. Flying in a level attitude back towards Meigs Field.

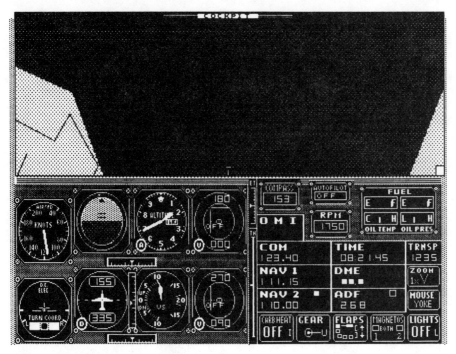

Fig. 2-8. Watching Meigs Field pass under the aircraft.

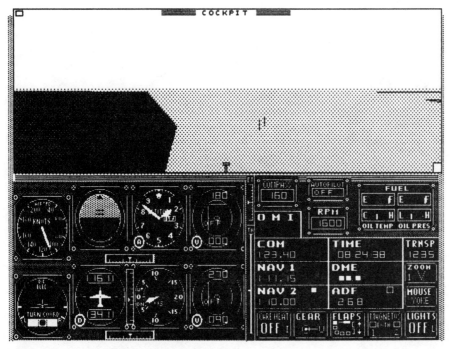

Fig. 2-9. Reducing the engine rpm and beginning a slow descent.

Step 9. At an altitude of 1500 feet, begin a right bank. Neutralize the ailerons/rudder combination. During the turn, slowly lower the throttle to 1500 rpm. Avoid using an excessive amount of down elevator at this time (Fig. 2-10).

Step 10. Make any necessary minor course adjustments for your final approach. Level the aircraft's wings. Line up with runway 36. Reduce the throttle to 800 rpm and lower the landing gear. Control the glide descent angle through small amounts of elevator pitch movements. Touch down (Fig. 2-11).

Flight Debriefing. If you successfully completed the following maneuvers, then you will have a passing grade for this flight:

☐ Take off on the described compass heading.
☐ Level the aircraft at 1000 feet.
☐ Complete a left bank.
☐ Complete a right bank.
☐ Land the aircraft on the specified runway.

GATES LEARJET ORIENTATION FLIGHT

Use the appropriate Flight Simulator starting method as discussed in Chapter 1. With the initial computer-oriented menu(s) correctly answered, begin the orientation flight setup.

Flight Setup. The environmental and reality factors will use the default settings.

Flight Objectives. Your goal during this flight is to successfully follow a 10-step orientation flight.

Filing the Flight Plan. Figure 2-12 is an aerial view of Oakland International Airport. At this time, your Gates Learjet is sitting on runway 27 Right. Your heading is 278 degrees. The fuel reading is full and the throttle is at 26 percent. The altimeter indicates an altitude of 7 feet. You have a forward view with a view magnification of 1×.

Step 1. Increase throttle to 100 percent and begin takeoff roll (Fig. 2-13).

Step 2. As your airspeed approaches 130 knots, give a slight amount of up elevator. Neutralize the elevator pitch when the aircraft rotates. Retract the landing gear (Fig. 2-14).

Step 3. At an altitude of 1000 feet, reduce the throttle to 80 percent. The aircraft will continue to climb (2-15).

Step 4. When the aircraft has reached an altitude of 3000 feet, reduce the throttle to 60 percent. Maintain an airspeed of at least 180 knots throughout these initial climbing maneuvers (Fig. 2-16).

Step 5. Begin a left bank. The current throttle setting could cause the aircraft to slip during this maneuver. Compensate for this altitude loss through a slight amount of up elevator (Fig. 2-17).

Step 6. Neutralize the bank on a heading of 80 degrees. Oakland International Airport is visible through the Forward View (Fig. 2-18).

Step 7. Switch to a Downward View. Watch for Oakland International Airport as the aircraft passes over its location (Fig. 2-19).

Step 8. Begin your landing descent. Use a slight amount of down elevator. Neutralize the descent at an altitude of 2500 feet (Fig. 2-20).

Step 9. Make a right bank. Watch your airspeed and altitude during this turn. Neutralize the bank on a heading of 270 degrees (Fig. 2-21).

Step 10. Make any necessary minor course adjustments for lining up on runway 27 Right. Level the aircraft. Reduce the throttle to 44 percent. Lower the landing gear. Control the glide descent angle through changes in the aircraft's elevator pitch. Touch down (Fig. 2-22).

Flight Debriefing. If you successfully completed the following maneuvers, then you will have a passing grade for this flight:

☐ Take off on the described compass heading.

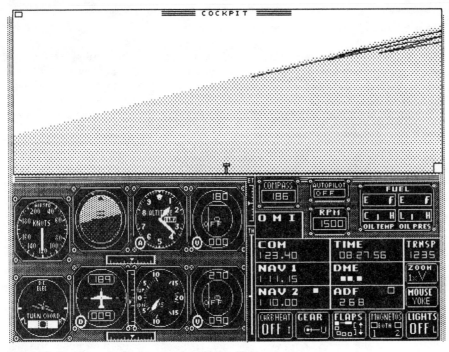

Fig. 2-10. Turning onto final approach to Meigs Field.

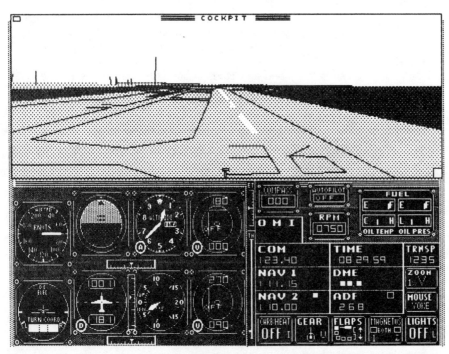

Fig. 2-11. The landing gear has been extended and the aircraft is gliding in for landing.

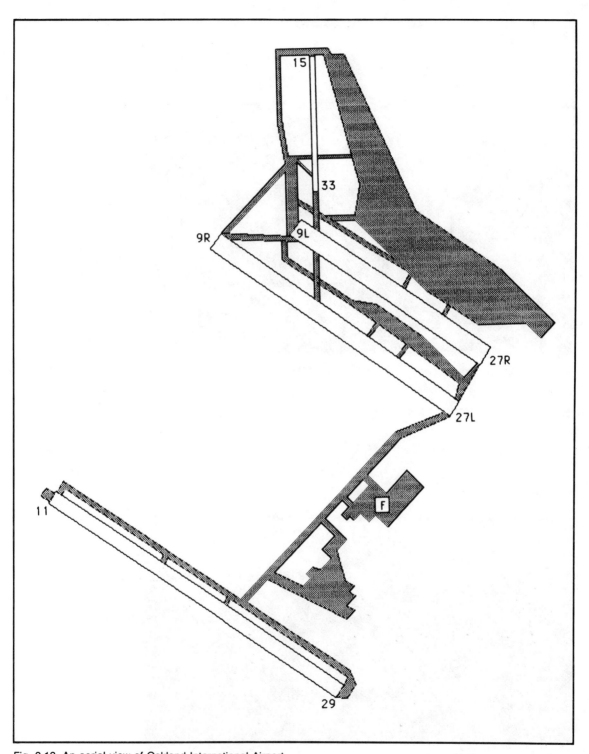

Fig. 2-12. An aerial view of Oakland International Airport.

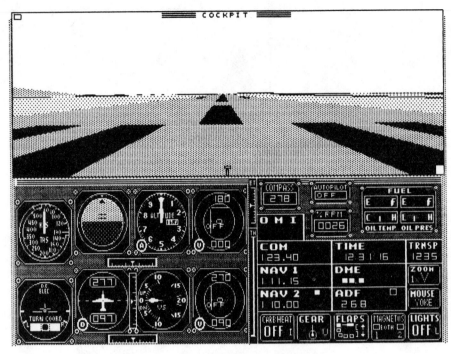

Fig. 2-13. Lined up ready for takeoff in a Gates Learjet 25G.

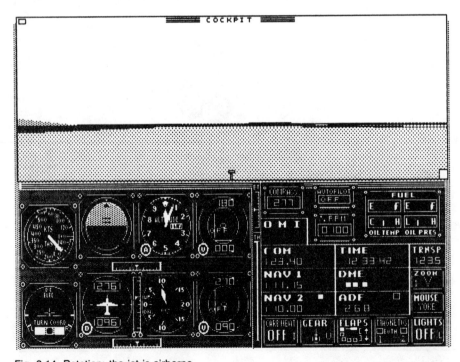

Fig. 2-14. Rotation; the jet is airborne.

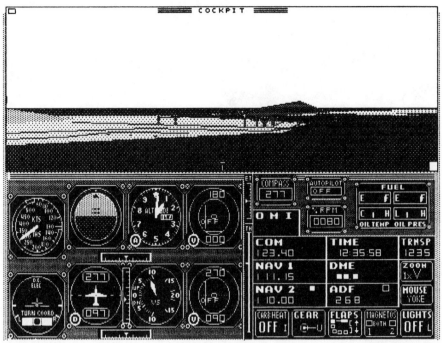

Fig. 2-15. The landing gear has been retracted and the aircraft is climbing using 80 percent engine power.

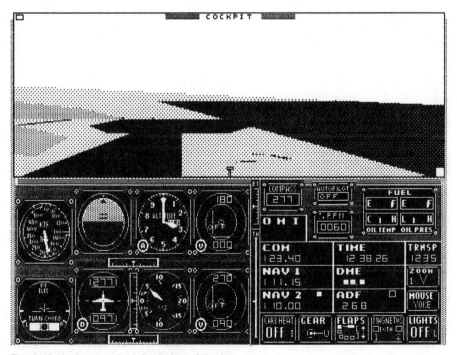

Fig. 2-16. A view out the left window of the jet.

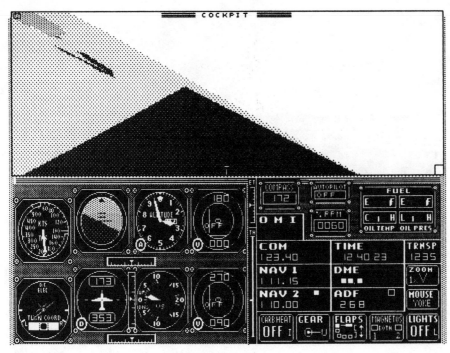

Fig. 2-17. A left bank turning the jet back towards OAK.

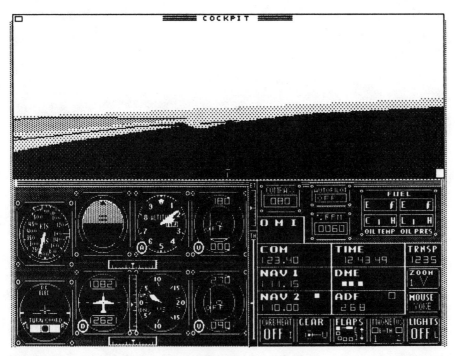

Fig. 2-18. Approaching OAK from the northwest.

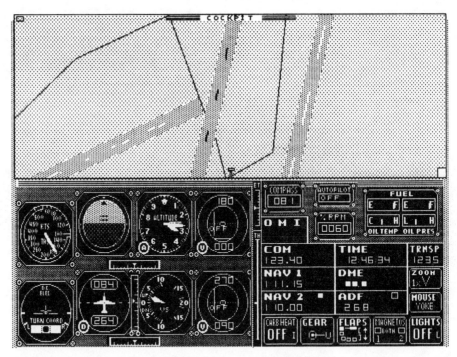

Fig. 2-19. Examining Oakland International Airport while flying over.

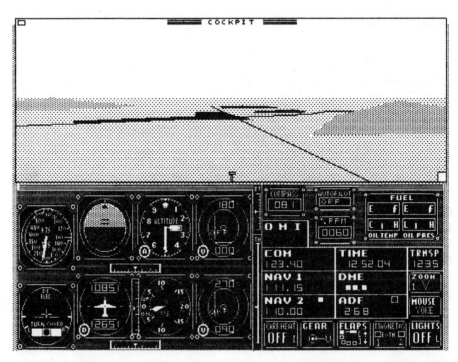

Fig. 2-20. Reducing power to 60 percent and beginning the descent into a landing posture.

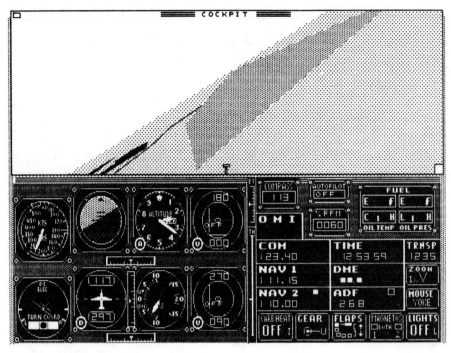

Fig. 2-21. Turning onto the final approach for runway 27 Right.

Fig. 2-22. A good smooth glide attitude with reduced power for landing at OAK.

□ Level the aircraft at 3000 feet.
□ Complete a left bank.
□ Complete a right bank.
□ Land the aircraft on the proper runway.

Now that you've had a taste of real simulator flying, it's time for a more extensive course in flight instruction.

Chapter 3

Flight Instruction

Learning the intricacies of flight can be an exacting process. Each flight—or, more likely, flight *attempt*—is fraught with potential aircraft and pilot disaster. All of these physical stresses and structural excesses are unnecessary. By using a planned and patient instructional technique, all of the Flight Simulator functions can be mastered in just four simple lessons.

These lessons take you from your beginning efforts at learning how to taxi the Cessna 182 around on the ground to recovering from a high-altitude, low-speed stall condition in the Gates Learjet. Each lesson is complete with a step-by-step guide for learning how to perform the particular flight maneuver. This step-by-step process can be repeated as many times as needed for gaining the degree of proficiency that is required for becoming a simulator pilot. At the conclusion of each lesson a competence test will evaluate your mastery of the instruction that has been presented in that particular lesson. Therefore, if you can pass all four lesson tests, then you will have absolutely no problem successfully soloing in the next chapter.

Flight Setup. The initial menu setup will be the same for all four of these lessons. The environmental and reality factors will use the default settings.

LESSON 1

Lesson Setup. If at any point during this lesson you crash the aircraft, just exit Flight Simulator and return to the startup screen.

Lesson Objectives. Learn to taxi, take off, and land the Cessna/Piper.

Performing the Lesson. You are starting on the runway of the default airport. This airport is Oakland International Airport with the 68000 versions and Meigs Field in Chicago, Illinois, for all other Flight Simulator versions. Your aircraft's throttle is idling at 650 rpm.

Taxi.

Step 1. Slowly increase the throttle to 800 rpm. Watch the airspeed indicator. You will start to move, as your airspeed increases.

Step 2. Turn on the aircraft's Radar or Map display. Adjust the magnification for a comfortable view of the aircraft taxiing along the runway. After you have examined the airport, switch back to the Forward View.

Step 3. Reduce the throttle back to its idle setting of 650 rpm. The aircraft will continue to roll. Apply the brakes to halt all movement.

Step 4. Once again, increase the throttle to 800 rpm. As the aircraft begins to roll, hold the ailerons/rudder combination in a hard right turn. The aircraft will quickly turn to the right. Neutralizing the ailerons/rudder will stop the turn.

Step 5. Practice several turns from both the cockpit Forward View and the overhead Radar display view.

Step 6. When you have finished your taxiing practice, reduce the throttle to 650 rpm and apply the brakes.

Three important points to remember when taxiing: use slow speeds, keep the throttle rpm to a minimum, and make all of your turns wide.

Taxi Test. Taxi the Cessna/Piper from its current position to the airport's fueling location. This site is designated by a large "F" inside a box.

You will receive a passing grade on this test if you can:

☐ Taxi to the fueling location.
☐ Stay on the airport's hard surfaces.

Take Off.

Step 1. Taxi to the center of the default airport's main runway.

Step 2. Slowly taxi the entire length of the runway at a reduced throttle of 800 rpm. Study the various landmarks along the length of the runway.

Step 3. Stop at the far end of the runway and turn to a new heading that is 180 degrees to your current heading. Keep the Cessna/Piper on the same runway that you just taxied down.

Step 4. Begin the takeoff roll. Slowly increase the throttle to 2200 rpm.

Step 5. As your airspeed reaches 60 knots, give some up elevator. Use two keystrokes of the up elevator key.

Step 6. When the nose of the aircraft clears the ground, neutralize the pitch (Fig. 3-1).

Step 7. Retract the landing gear and reduce the throttle to 1750 rpm.

Takeoff Test. Use each of the airport's runways (Meigs Field has one runway, while Oakland International Airport has four) and take off from each direction.

You will receive a passing grade on this test if you can:

☐ Make a smooth and steady rate of climb during takeoff.
☐ Raise the landing gear.
☐ Reduce the throttle following the retraction of the landing gear.

Landing.

Step 1. Taxi onto one of the airport's main runways (remember Meigs Field only has one runway).

Step 2. Line up in the center of the runway.

Step 3. Begin takeoff roll. Increase throttle to 2200 rpm.

Step 4. Give a slight amount of up elevator. Use two up elevator keystrokes.

Step 5. As the nose leaves the ground, neutralize the pitch. When you are airborne, retract the landing gear and reduce the throttle to 1750 rpm.

Step 6. Level the aircraft at an altitude of 1K by using slight down elevator.

Step 7. Bank to the left. Reduce the throttle to 1600 rpm while in the bank.

Step 8. Level the aircraft. Line up on one of the airport's runways. Make any necessary minor course adjustments.

Step 9. Lower the landing gear. Reduce the throttle to 800 rpm.

Step 10. Give a slight down elevator. Use two down elevator keystrokes.

Step 11. At an altitude of 80 feet above the runway (*Note*: this is not the true altimeter reading), start bringing the nose up with small amounts of up elevator and neutralize the pitch.

Step 12. Place the nose of the aircraft on a spot at the far end of the runway.

Step 13. Watch your airspeed. Maintain an airspeed of approximately 70 to 80 knots.

Step 14. Glide over the near end of the runway with the angle of descent intersecting the middle of the runway (Fig. 3-2). Use one press of the up elevator key and don't neutralize the pitch.

Step 15. Touch down.

Landing Test. Make a landing on all of the airport's runways, taxi off of each runway, and taxi to the fueling location.

You will receive a passing grade on this test if you can:

☐ Line up on the proper runway.
☐ Reduce throttle for a slow approach.
☐ Lower the landing gear.
☐ Land on the runway.

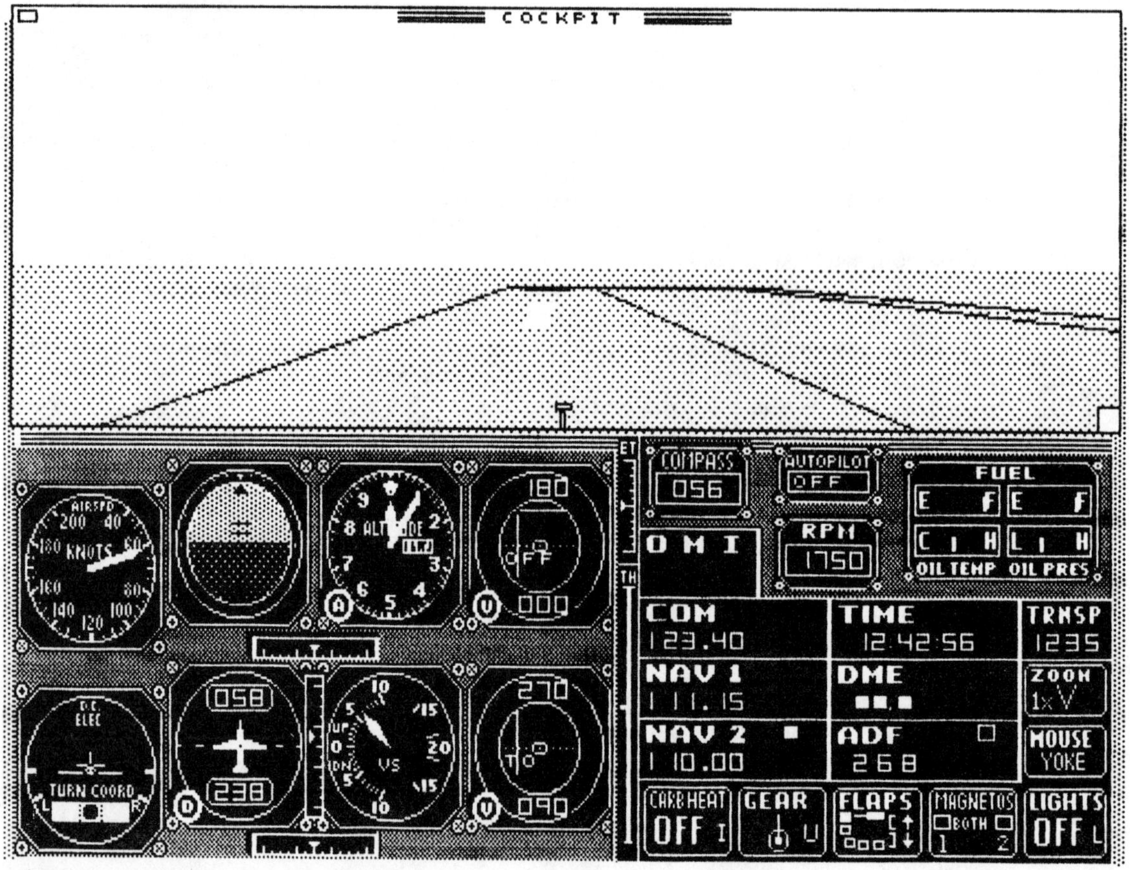

Fig. 3-1. Leaving the runway on a typical takeoff.

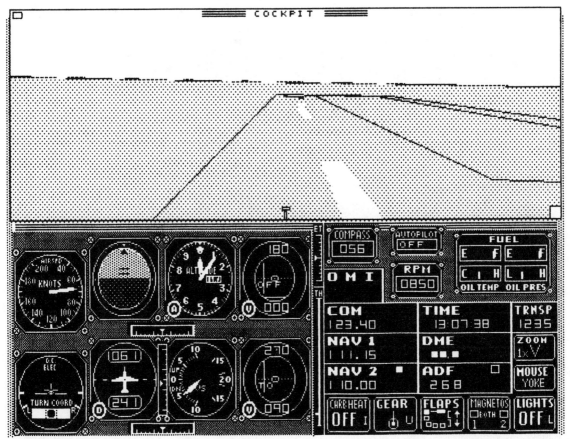

Fig. 3-2. A slow, steady descent is the key to a good landing. In this case, a low throttle setting helps to reduce the aircraft's speed.

LESSON 2

Lesson Setup. If at any point during this lesson you crash the aircraft, just exit Flight Simulator and return to the startup screen.

Lesson Objectives. Learn to change altitude and alter airspeed in the Cessna, Piper, and Gates Learjet.

Performing the Lesson. If you elect to practice this lesson in the Gates Learjet, remember to alter the airspeed and throttle settings so that they correspond with the performance specifications for this jet aircraft.

Altitude Change.

Step 1. Take off.

Step 2. Keep the throttle setting at 2200 rpm and retract the landing gear.

Step 3. Continue to climb to an altitude of 5000 feet. The rate of climb should be both slow and steady.

Step 4. At an altitude of 5000 feet, reduce the throttle to 1750 rpm. Continue the climb.

Step 5. Level the aircraft at 10,000 feet. Use a slight amount of down elevator pitch.

Step 6. Using a Pilot Mode viewpoint, examine all of the view directions.

Step 7. Bank left. Neutralize the bank. Continue the bank to a new heading that is 180 degrees from your present heading. When the new heading is reached, level the aircraft.

Step 8. Pitch the aircraft's nose down. Use four keystrokes of the down elevator. Neutralize the pitch. Watch the Airspeed Indicator during this dive.

Step 9. Level the aircraft when an altitude of 1000 feet is reached.

Step 10. Compensate for any loss in altitude with a slight amount of up elevator.

Altitude Change Test. Climb to an altitude of 12,000 feet. Reduce throttle to 1600 rpm and dive to an altitude of 2000 feet. At the same throttle setting, climb back to an altitude of 8,500 feet.

You will receive a passing grade on this test if you can:

☐ Execute a climb.
☐ Execute a dive.
☐ Prevent aircraft stress and avoid stalls or a crash.

Alter Airspeed.

Step 1. Take off.

Step 2. Keep the throttle setting at 2200 rpm and retract the landing gear.

Step 3. Climb to an altitude of 500 feet and level the aircraft.

Step 4. Watch the indicated airspeed climb. At a speed of 110 knots, reduce the throttle to 1750 rpm.

Step 5. Climb to an altitude of 1000 feet.

Step 6. Bank to the left. At a new heading that is 90 degrees from your present heading, level the aircraft.

Step 7. Increase the throttle to 2500 rpm.

Step 8. Climb to an altitude of 12,000 feet. Level the aircraft at 12,000 feet.

Step 9. Reduce the throttle to 1750 rpm.

Step 10. Pitch the aircraft's nose down with three keystrokes. Neutralize the pitch.

Step 11. Observe the indicated airspeed.

Step 12. Level the aircraft at an altitude of 1000 feet.

Step 13. Increase the throttle to 2500 rpm. Watch the rate of fuel consumption.

Step 14. After a noticeable loss of fuel, increase the throttle to full power and watch the rate of fuel consumption.

Airspeed Test. At a fixed throttle of 1600 rpm, fluctuate the airspeed between 80 and 140 knots without increasing the throttle setting.

You will receive a passing grade on this test if you can:

☐ Control the aircraft's airspeed, altitude, and attitude through a fixed throttle control.

LESSON 3

Lesson Setup. If at any point during this lesson you crash the aircraft, just exit Flight Simulator and return to the startup screen.

Lesson Objectives. Learn three maneuvers. Each maneuver is indicated below in italic type.

Performing the Lesson. If you elect to practice this lesson in the Gates Learjet, remember to alter the airspeed and throttle settings so that they correspond with the performance specifications for this jet aircraft.

Maneuvers.

Step 1. Take off.

Step 2. Retract landing gear, but keep the throttle setting at 2200 rpm.

Step 3. Climb to an altitude of 12,000 feet.

Step 4. Level the aircraft at an altitude of 12,000 feet. Reduce the throttle to 2000 rpm.

Step 5. *Bank* to the right. Neutralize the bank. Increase the throttle to 2500 rpm.

Step 6. Keep the aircraft in this attitude and make several complete 360 degree circles.

Step 7. Level the aircraft. Reduce the throttle to 1600 rpm.

Step 8. *Bank* to the left. Neutralize the bank. Keep throttle at 1600 rpm.

Step 9. Keep the aircraft in this attitude and make several complete 360 degree circles (Fig. 3-3). Notice the drop in the indicated airspeed. When the airspeed reaches 70 knots, the aircraft will start to lose altitude.

Step 10. Level the aircraft.

Step 11. *Roll* right. Press and hold the right aileron key. Watch the Airspeed Indicator.

Step 12. After several revolutions, use the appropriate aileron keystroke to stop and level the aircraft. Compensate for any loss in altitude and climb back to an altitude of 12,000 feet.

Step 13. Increase the throttle to 2500 rpm.

Step 14. *Loop* the aircraft. Begin a shallow dive. At an indicated airspeed of 190 knots, press and hold the up elevator key. Avoid too much up elevator or a "false" stall may occur. The indicated airspeed will drop and the horizon will slowly appear along the top of the canopy. Continue to hold the up elevator (follow the above false stall reminder). The aircraft will slowly pitch up until the true horizon once again appears. At this point, neutralize the pitch and level the aircraft.

High-Speed Maneuvers Test. Climb to an altitude of 8,000 feet and do one roll, bank 360 degrees to the left, level the aircraft, do three rolls to the right, level the aircraft, bank 360 degrees

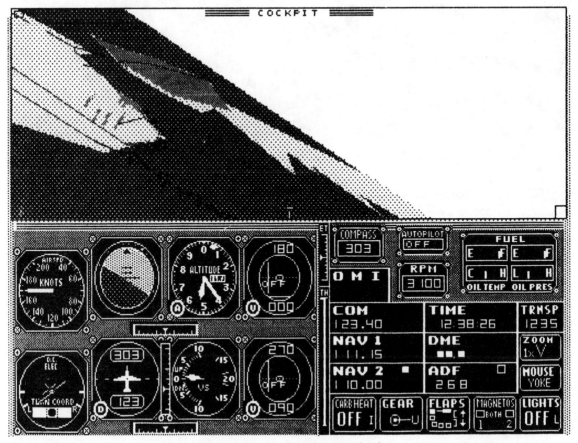

Fig. 3-3. The aircraft's rpm have increased during this high-performance bank.

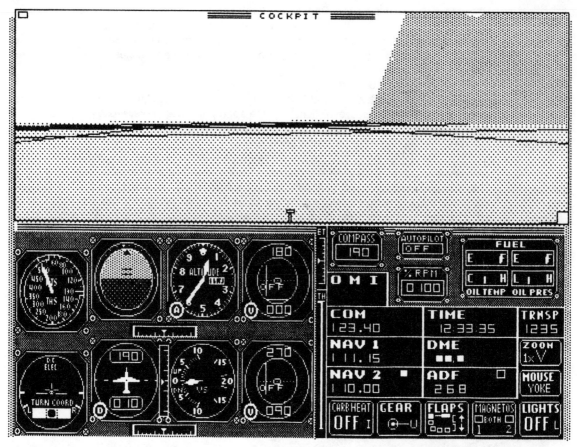

Fig. 3-4. High-speed, low-level flight in the Gates Learjet 25G is a demanding task that requires a light touch on the control yoke.

to the right, level the aircraft, execute six rolls to the left, level the aircraft, and do two consecutive loops.You will receive a passing grade on this test if you can:

☐ Do the correct number of iterations for each maneuver.
☐ Avoid any excessive loss in altitude.
☐ Perform all of the maneuvers without either stressing or crashing the aircraft (Fig. 3-4).

LESSON 4

Lesson Setup. If at any point during this lesson you crash the aircraft, just exit Flight Simulator and return to the startup screen.

Lesson Objectives. Practice emergency flight procedures for the Cessna, Piper, and Gates Learjet. These are all potentially lifesaving lessons that might come in handy during Part II's historical aviation scenarios.

Performing the Lesson.
Emergency Procedures.
Half-Power Takeoff.
Step 1. Assume a standard takeoff posture.

Step 2. Increase throttle to 1750 rpm.

Step 3. Follow a standard takeoff roll.

Zero Throttle on Landing.

Step 1. Line up for a standard landing.

Step 2. At an altitude of 1000 feet, reduce the throttle to its idle setting (650 rpm).

Step 3. Avoid raising the nose of the aircraft for alignment with the far end of the runway.

Step 4. Follow a typical landing, but don't lower the landing gear until the aircraft is over the edge of the runway threshold.

Step 5. At the edge of the runway, lower the landing gear.

Step 6. Touch down.

Stall.

Step 1. Climb to an altitude of 9000 feet.

Step 2. Reduce the throttle to 1000 rpm.

Step 3. When the airspeed has dropped to 100 knots, try to loop the aircraft.

Step 4. The aircraft will stall. Immediately neutralize the pitch.

Step 5. Point the aircraft's nose towards the ground and level the aircraft (i.e., counteract any spinning, rolling, or rotation).

Step 6. As the indicated airspeed increases (above 100 knots), slowly give a slight amount of up elevator. Neturalize the pitch.

Step 7. Level the aircraft.

High-Speed, Low-Altitude Flight.

Step 1. Level the aircraft at an altitude of 500 feet.

Step 2. Increase the throttle to 2500 rpm.

Step 3. Bank to the left. Neutralize the bank.

Step 4. After a bank of 360 degrees, level the aircraft.

Step 5. Reduce the aircraft's altitude to 200 feet and repeat the above bank.

Step 6. Reduce the aircraft's altitude to 100 feet and execute the same bank.

High-Speed, Small Radius Turn.

Step 1. Climb to an altitude of 7500 feet.

Step 2. Increase the throttle to 2500 rpm.

Step 3. At an indicated airspeed of 140 knots, bank to the right. Neutralize the bank.

Step 4. In order to reduce the turning radius, slowly give a slight amount of up elevator. Neutralize the pitch.

Step 5. Watch the Airspeed Indicator, the Altimeter, and the Heading Indicator.

Step 6. Before the aircraft stalls, level the aircraft and neutralize all of the controls.

Half-Runway Takeoff.

Step 1. Taxi to the midpoint of the default airport's main runway.

Step 2. Apply full throttle (2500 rpm).

Step 3. When the indicated airspeed reaches 70 knots, give a slight amount of up elevator.

Full Power Landing.

Step 1. Assume a standard landing approach.

Step 2. Keep the throttle fixed at 2200 rpm.

Step 3. Lower the landing gear. Apply a full 40 degrees worth of flaps. This will increase both lift and drag.

Step 4. Avoid any excessive aircraft pitch.

Step 5. Fly the aircraft onto the runway. Immediately cut the throttle to 650 rpm when the Altimeter shows that you have landed.

Tarmac Takeoff.

Step 1. Taxi off the runway and onto one of the airport's tarmac regions.

Step 2. Assume a standard takeoff posture.

Step 3. Increase the throttle to 2500 rpm.

Step 4. When the indicated airspeed reaches 70 knots, give a slight amount of up elevator. Neutralize the pitch.

Step 5. Follow the rest of the standard takeoff procedure.

Gates Learjet—Specific Emergency Procedures.

Full-Power Landing.

Step 1. Assume a standard landing approach.

Step 2. Keep the throttle fixed at 60 percent.

Step 3. Lower the landing gear and apply a full 40 degrees worth of flaps.

Step 4. Avoid any excessive aircraft pitch. Using flaps at high speeds will cause the nose of the jet to pitch down. Counteract this tendency with a slight amount of up elevator.

Step 5. Fly the jet directly onto the runway. Reduce the throttle to 26 percent immediately after touchdown. The Gates Learjet has tremendous gliding capabilities. Therefore, mark your descent angle intersection with the near end of the runway. This will give you plenty of room for settling onto the runway.

Stall.

Step 1. Climb to an altitude of 25,000 feet.

Step 2. Reduce the throttle to 45 percent.

Step 3. When the airspeed has dropped to 140 knots, try to loop the aircraft.

Step 4. The aircraft will stall. Immediately neutralize the pitch.

Step 5. Point the aircraft's nose towards the ground and level the aircraft (i.e., counteract any spinning, rolling, or rotation).

Step 6. As the indicated airspeed increases (above 150 knots), slowly give a slight amount of up elevator. Neutralize the pitch.

Step 7. Level the aircraft.

High-Speed, Small Radius Turn.

Step 1. Climb to an altitude of 10,000 feet.

Step 2. Increase the throttle to 100 percent.

Step 3. At an indicated airspeed of 300 knots, bank to the right. Neutralize the bank.

Step 4. In order to reduce the turning radius, slowly give a slight amount of up elevator. Neutralize the pitch.

Step 5. Watch the Airspeed Indicator, the Altimeter, and the Heading Indicator.

Step 6. Before the aircraft stalls, level the aircraft and neutralize all of the controls.

Emergency Procedure Test. Successfully perform all of these emergency procedures by using different test criteria. For example, try different altitudes, attitudes, and airspeeds during each emergency procedure.

You will receive a passing grade on this test if you can:

☐ Understand the physical properties behind the operation of each emergency procedure.

☐ Perform any procedure under a wide variety of different conditions.

☐ Execute each procedure without suffering any aircraft damage or pilot loss.

Chapter 4

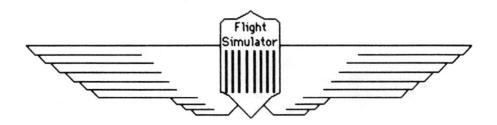

Solo Flight

Now that you have completed both your basic and advanced flight instruction, it is time to test your competence in handling your aircraft. The following two tests will push your physical and mental abilities to their limits. If you are able to successfully complete both of these flight tests, then you can consider yourself to have graduated with honors from the Flight Simulator flight school. Make sure that you have passed these tests and earned your wings before you attempt any of the historical aviation scenarios that are contained in Part II. It is far better to evaluate your level of flying proficiency at this time than later, when Roscoe Turner and Amelia Earhart are trying to edge you out of the 1935 Bendix Trophy Race.

Cessna/Piper Flight Test Setup. If you should crash your aircraft during this test, just exit Flight Simulator and return to the startup screen.

The environmental and reality factors will use the default settings.

Test Objectives. Test the aircraft handling proficiency of the Flight Simulator pilot.

Taking the Test.

Step 1. Take off from the main runway.

Step 2. Climb to an altitude of 6750 feet with an indicated airspeed of 80 knots.

Step 3. Accelerate to an indicated airspeed of 120 knots.

Step 4. Climb to an altitude of 9000 feet and accelerate to 130 knots.

Step 5. Assume a new heading of 313 degrees and reduce airspeed to 110 knots.

Step 6. Climb to an altitude of 10,000 feet. Turn to a heading of 215 degrees.

Step 7. Reduce your altitude to 7500 feet.

Step 8. Reduce throttle to 650 rpm.

Step 9. Pitch the aircraft's nose up 90 degrees.

Step 10. Neutralize the pitch.

Step 11. Recover from the stall at an altitude of 1000 feet.

Step 12. Turn to a new heading of 180 degrees.

Step 13. Increase the throttle to cruising speed.

Step 14. Make a landing approach on the main runway.

Step 15. Perform a touch-and-go landing on the runway.

Step 16. Climb to an altitude of 1,000 feet.

Step 17. Make a bank to the right on a new heading of 100 degrees.

Step 18. Cross over the airport at an altitude of 500 feet with a heading of 270 degrees.

Step 19. By using your cockpit instruments only, execute a left bank. Level the aircraft in a normal flight attitude on a heading of 0 degrees.

Step 20. Switch back to VFR conditions. Land on the main runway and park at the airport's fueling location.

Test Debriefing. You will receive a passing grade on this test if you:

☐ Performed each maneuver perfectly.
☐ Didn't overtax either the airframe or the pilot.
☐ Landed the Cessna/Piper with an elapsed time of under 15 minutes.

Certificate of Flight Simulator Solo Flight

This is to acknowledge that,

did professionally and competently pass the rigorous Flight Simulator solo flight course on

Possession of this certificate grants the bearer the right to fly a piston-powered or jet aircraft in any historical aviation scenario.

Fig. 4-1. After you have successfully completed the solo flight test, place your name and the day's date on this certificate.

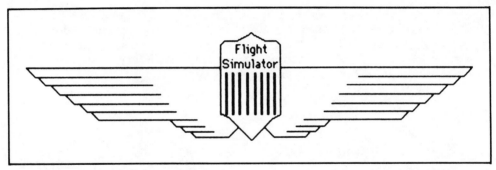

Fig. 4-2. As an acknowledgment of your soloing, cut these wings from this book and pin them to the front of your shirt. Wear them proudly.

Gates Learjet Flight Test Setup. If you should crash your aircraft during this test, just exit Flight Simulator and return to the startup screen.

The environmental and reality factors will use the default settings.
You will be using the Oakland International Airport during this test.
Test Objectives. Test the jet handling proficiency of the Flight Simulator pilot.
Taking the Test.
Step 1. Take off from the runway with 49 percent thrust.
Step 2. Climb to an altitude of 6,000 feet and accelerate to an indicated airspeed of 200 knots.
Step 3. Accelerate to an indicated airspeed of 300 knots.
Step 4. Climb to an altitude of 10,000 feet and accelerate to 400 knots.
Step 5. Assume a new heading of 350 degrees and reduce airspeed to 200 knots.
Step 6. Climb to an altitude of 12,000 feet. Turn to a heading of 265 degrees.
Step 7. Reduce your altitude to 8,750 feet.
Step 8. Reduce throttle to 26 percent.
Step 9. Pitch the aircraft's nose up 90 degrees.
Step 10. Neutralize the pitch.
Step 11. Recover from the stall at an altitude of 1000 feet.
Step 12. Turn to a new heading of 111 degrees.
Step 13. Increase the throttle to cruising speed.
Step 14. Make a landing approach on runway 9 Left.
Step 15. Perform a touch-and-go landing on the runway.
Step 16. Climb to an altitude of 1,000 feet.
Step 17. Bank to the left on a new heading of 0 degrees.
Step 18. Fly over the airport at an altitude of 500 feet on a heading of 180 degrees.
Step 19. Turn to a heading of 85 degrees.
Step 20. Land on runway 27 Left. Park at the airport's fueling location.
Test Debriefing. You will receive a passing grade on this test if you:

☐ Performed each maneuver perfectly.
☐ Didn't overtax either the airframe or the pilot.
☐ Landed the Gates Learjet with an elapsed time under 15 minutes.

Once you have passed both of these tests, your flying competence in both a modern piston-powered aircraft and a contemporary business jet is beyond reproach. Interestingly enough, much of the material from both of these tests is exactly duplicated from an actual pilot testing program. Therefore, your flight simulation skill is steeped in genuine performance criteria.

Only two final duties await your attention before proceeding to the aerial escapades contained in Part II. First, the Flight Graduation Citation in Fig. 4-1 should be completed with your name. After all, you earned it. Second, lacking a full-scale ceremony, make a copy of the wings insignia in Figure 4-2. Then pin this most prestigious of pilot awards to the front of your flight suit. Wear them proudly as you fly the following historical aviation scenarios.

Part 2
Historical Aviation Scenarios

A marvelous attribute of Flight Simulator is its ability to recreate virtually any historical aircraft activity from the annals of aviation history. Almost any event can be thoroughly and realistically represented through the manipulation of the Cessna, Piper, and Gates Learjet silhouettes and their associated flight parameters. Throw in a modest amount of imagination and you will soon be flying a Wright Pusher EX across the country on the dangerous *Vin Fiz* tour, or making the inaugural flight of the Douglas DC-9 in late 1965.

In the following nine chapters, the most exciting and memorable aerial activities from 1903 to the present day are carefully recreated for use with Flight Simulator. Each chapter depicts several historical events that have been fully documented to ensure their adherence to fact. In other words, throttle settings, altimeter readings, and indicated airspeeds have all been painstakingly researched for an exact duplication of the performance specifications that are represented by the aircraft from each particular scenario. Additionally, if the pilot of the actual historical aircraft performed a successful flight, then you too will be expected to match this feat. All in all, you will witness the thrill of flying in a real-life situation without suffering the discomfort of losing your life.

The format used in each of these historical scenarios is similar to the structure that was used in the previous instructional chapters. Following a brief historical introduction to the events surrounding the scenario, the **Flight Setup** steps through the required conditions that existed at the time of the actual flight. For example, weather factors and aircraft trustworthiness will be listed in this section. Armed with this data, you will then use the built-in Flight Simulator editor for modifying the default settings to match these flight conditions.

Using this editor is remarkably easy. A special keystroke is used for placing the editor on the computer's monitor (the Menu Bar on the 68000 versions replaces the need for this special keystroke). From this position, numerous flight control parameters can be modified to satisfy any type of situation. There are simulation factors, aircraft positioning controls, and environmental conditions on the editor menu. You can even use the editor for saving each of the historical aviation scenarios on a separate floppy disk. Each of these attributes can be altered to a wide range of different values. This flexibility lends itself to meeting the diverse demands that are presented in the **Flight Setup** section of each scenario.

Then, with your aircraft ready to go, the **Flight Objectives** are outlined. These are the goals that should be met for successfully completing the scenario. Next, **Filing the Flight Plan** gives a short step-by-step accounting of the procedure that should be used for achieving the mission objectives. Finally, the **Flight Debriefing** grades your performance in meeting the flight's objectives.

Each scenario is self-contained; only the Flight Simulator software is necessary for satisfying the flight objectives. In spite of this predominant reliance on the master flight simulation software, many of the scenarios list the optional subLOGIC Scenery Disks in the **Flight Setup** section. For the most part, subLOGIC Scenery Disks will greatly enhance the realism of each scenario. Therefore, if you have access to this special software package, use it. Otherwise, fly the scenario from any location where you feel most comfortable.

Those pilots who lack the Scenery Disks can still find plenty of action in Chapters 6, 10, 11, and 13. None of the scenarios in these four chapters use any outside geographical locations. In fact, three of the four (6, 10, and 11) rely totally on the WWI Ace mode found in Flight Simulator.

Flying the 30 combat scenarios in Chapters 6, 10, and 11 provides an interesting diversion from the tense, competitive action found in the other sections. Like their pacifist cousins, however, each of these aerial warfare vignettes has a rigid set of mission objectives. Meeting these objectives while staying within the boundaries of the mission setup parameters could prove more difficult than breaking the 1923 speed record.

Finally, there are two Appendices that will increase your enjoyment of these scenarios: the Aircraft Indentification Guide (Appendix C) and the Aviation Time Line (Appendix D). These two appendices contain facts that will help place each scenario in a proper historical perspective and provide some additional data about the aircraft you are flying.

Chapter 5

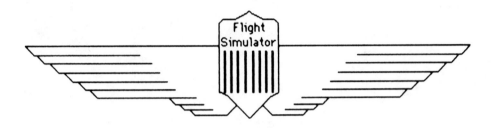

Early Flight

1. 17 DECEMBER 1903

Two young inventors, Wilbur and Orville Wright (Wilbur was the senior by four years), from New Castle, Indiana (Wilbur), and Dayton, Ohio (Orville), began to apply their rich mechanical talents towards a solution for manned flight in 1896. This date coincided with the death of the German glider pioneer Otto Lilienthal. Slowly their early experimentation took on a more serious thrust, with their bicycle business becoming a secondary interest. After building and flying several large kites, the brothers wanted to expand their flight tests with large manned gliders. By studying the weather conditions of several potential test sites, Wilbur and Orville established a small section of sandy beach near Kitty Hawk, North Carolina, an area known as Kill Devil Hill, as their permanent test center. Following three years of extensive glider flights, the brothers developed an ambitious design based on a powered glider or airplane. Costing less than $1000 to build, the Wright Flyer had a four-cylinder 12-horsepower gasoline engine mounted on a standard glider airframe. The planned test flight was set for September 1903, but a series of weather problems delayed the initial flight until December of the same year. With Wilbur at the controls, the Wright Flyer made its first flight attempt on 14 December 1903. Unfortunately, bad judgement on Wilbur's part stalled the aircraft and it crashed. Four days later it was Orville's turn. Traveling at a speed of 5.9 knots, Orville made the first manned aircraft flight on 17 December 1903. The total distance covered on this epic voyage was approximately 100 feet with a duration of 12 seconds. The age of flight had been born.

Flight Setup.
Auto-coordination—Off.
Reality mode—On.
Time: Hours—10. Minutes—35.
Season—Winter.
Cloud layer 1 tops—3000.
Cloud layer 1 bottoms—2000.

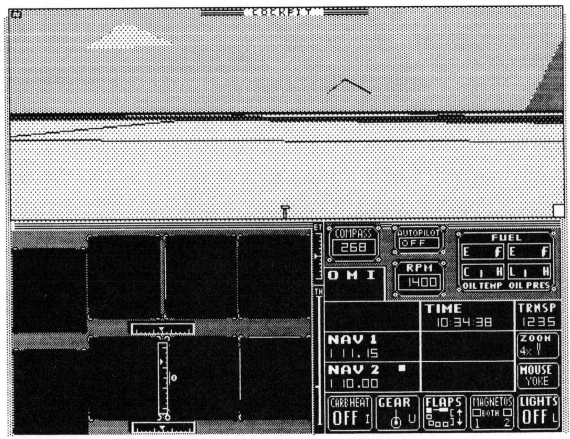

Fig. 5-1. Using no cockpit instrumentation and a minimal engine throttle setting, this Cessna is simulating the historic December flight of the Wrights.

Surface wind: Knots—19. Degrees—220.

Reliability factor—90.

No cockpit instruments are available on the Wright Flyer.

Flight Objectives. Duplicate the initial Wright flight.

Filing the Flight Plan.

Step 1. Start the engine.

Step 2. Taxi the aircraft to a takeoff heading of 220. (For greater realism, use: 14923N 20819E Alt.—413, as Kill Devil Hill, NC from Scenery Disk 7.)

Step 3. Fix the throttle at 1450 rpm. (It is impossible to exactly duplicate the performance specifications of the Wright 1903 Flyer with the Cessna or Piper.)

Step 4. Begin the takeoff roll.

Step 5. Take off and fly 100 feet (Fig. 5-1).

Step 6. Land safely and taxi back to the airport's fueling location.

Flight Debriefing. You will have successfully completed this flight if you:

☐ Followed the performance specifications of the Wright 1903 Flyer.

☐ Flew the aircraft for 100 feet.

☐ Safely return the aircraft to *terra firma.*

2. SPEED RECORD 1906

Alberto Santos-Dumont set Europe's first speed record by flying his Santos-Dumont 14-bis to 22.281 knots on 12 November 1906.

Flight Setup.

Auto-coordination—Off.

Reality mode—On.

Time: Hours—11. Minutes—00.

Season—Fall.

Surface wind: Knots—5. Degrees—300.

Reliability factor—80.

No cockpit instruments are available on the Santos-Dumont 14-bis.

Flight Objectives. Break the 1906 speed record.

Filing the Flight Plan.

Step 1. Start the engine. (Use: 17417N 7446E Alt.—416 as your starting location.)

Step 2. Keep the engine throttle below 1450 rpm.

Step 3. Take off. Stay below an altitude of 100 feet.

Step 4. Assume a straight and level flight. You must fly faster than 22 knots. Hold this speed for one minute.

Step 5. Return to the runway and land.

Step 6. Taxi to the airport's fueling location.

Flight Debriefing. You will have successfully completed this flight if you:

☐ Broke the 1906 speed record.
☐ Safely completed the flight.

3. *VIN FIZ*

Thriving on the sensational, William Randolph Hearst made an offer that few aviators could refuse. In 1911, Hearst offered a prize of $50,000 to the first person who could fly an aircraft across the United States in 30 days or less. Several pilots entered this competition, but only one presented a solid attempt at winning the prize money.

Calbraith Perry Rodgers, who had only learned to fly a few months prior to this transcontinental attempt, obtained a new Wright EX for his steed in this race. Trying to defray the enormous expense that would be incurred from a flight across the United States, Rodgers enlisted the aid of a wealthy sponsor. Armour Company of Chicago agreed to pay Rodgers $5 for every mile that he flew, as long as his aircraft carried the logo for their new grape soft drink, which was named "Vin Fiz." With such professional backing, the Hearst prize money appeared in serious jeopardy of being won.

Rodgers began his race for the west coast on 17 September 1911. Taking off from Sheepshead Bay, Long Island, Rodgers elected to follow the railway system as a navigational aid. Thoughtfully, Armour Company supplied a private train for carrying spare parts, a team of mechanics, Rodgers' wife, and his mother. Both the rail navigation system and the special train turned out to be the undoing of Rodgers transcontinental attempt. On the morning of 18 September, *Vin Fiz* had its first in a number of time-consuming crashes. After a three-day delay, Rodgers somehow followed the wrong railway line and landed in Scranton, PA.

Plagued by such bad luck, the 30-day Hearst time limit expired with Rodgers flying over Oklahoma. Nevertheless, Rodgers exhibited true determination and elected to complete the cross-country trip anyway. On 5 November 1911, Rodgers landed at Pasadena, California. His actual flying time had been a remarkable 82 hours and 2 minutes.

Flight Setup.
Auto-coordination—Off.
Reality mode—On.
Time: Hours—8. Minutes—00.
Season—Fall.
Reliability factor—50.
No cockpit instruments are available on the Wright EX.

Flight Objectives. Fly Rodgers' course from Sheepshead Bay, Long Island, to Pasadena, California, in 82 hours and 2 minutes.

Filing the Flight Plan.
Step 1. Start the engine. Fix the throttle at 1450 rpm.
Step 2. Take off from John F. Kennedy International Airport; 17034N 21065E Alt.—12. (You may want to use the slewing controls for moving across the country.)
Step 3. Land in Pasadena, CA. (Use Riverside; 15284N 6143E Alt.—817.)

Flight Debriefing. You will have successfully completed this flight if you:

☐ Flew across the United States along a route similar to Rodgers'.
☐ Safely completed the cross-country journey. The only real physical injury that Rodgers suffered was a broken ankle at the end of his flight.

4. STINSON SOLO

Following in the wake of Rodgers' *Vin Fiz* cross-country flight, hundreds of people flocked to local flying schools in the hope of learning to fly. These determined aviators included both men and women. One of the earliest of the female pilots was Katherine Stinson. Prior to her 17th birthday, Katherine soloed at Max Lillie's flight school at Cicero Field in Chicago, Illinois. Armed with her flight certification and a sizable loan from her mother, Katherine purchased a used Wright Model B and began to tour county fairs. Her agent, Bill Pickins, gave Katherine $500 for each fair flight. This fame and fortune influenced Katherine's sister, Majorie, to attend the Wright flight school in Dayton, Ohio.

Flight Setup.
Auto-coordination—Off.
Reality mode—On.
Time: Hours—9. Minutes—00.
Season—Summer.
Reliability factor—80.
No cockpit instruments are available on the Partridge/Kelbr biplane.

Flight Objectives. Loop Katherine Stinson's Partridge/Keller biplane.

Filing the Flight Plan.
Step 1. Start the engine. Fix the throttle at 1450 rpm.

Step 2. Take off from Chicago-Midway Airport; 17156N 16628E Alt.—619.
Step 3. Loop the Partridge/Keller biplane.
Flight Debriefing. You will have successfully completed this flight if you:

☐ Executed one loop.
☐ Safely landed the aircraft. Katherine Stinson was the fourth American and the first woman to complete the loop manuever.

5. ALTITUDE RECORD 1913

M. Perreyon piloted a Bleriot Type XII to an altitude record of 19,291 feet on 11 March 1913.
Flight Setup.
Auto-coordination—Off.
Reality mode—On.
Time: Hours—8. Minutes—00.
Season—Spring.
Reliability factor—80.
Only the Airspeed Indicator and the Altimeter may be used on the Bleriot Type XII.
Flight Objectives. Break the 1913 altitude record.
Filing the Flight Plan.
Step 1. Start the engine. (Use: 17417N 7446E Alt.—416 as your starting location.)
Step 2. Keep the engine throttle below 1450 rpm.
Step 3. Take off. Climb to an altitude higher than the 1913 record.
Step 4. Fly in a level attitude at the new altitude and hold your speed for one minute.
Step 5. Return to the runway and land.
Flight Debriefing. You will have successfully completed this flight if you:

☐ Broke the 1913 altitude record.
☐ Safely completed the flight.

Chapter 6

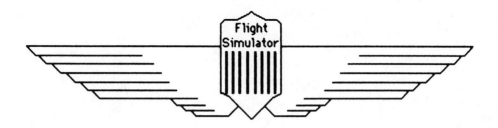

World War I

6. ITALO-TURKISH WAR

Faced with an Arab-Turkish occupation of Tripoli, Libya, Italy sent an invasion force to Libya under the pretext of protecting Italians living in this coastal city. Accompanying the more conventional task force was a new armed service branch known as the Air Flotilla. Commanded by Captain Carlos Piazza, the Air Flotilla had a strength of five pilots, six reserve pilots, 30 mechanics, and nine operational aircraft. The battle for Tripoli, which began on 5 October 1911, lasted 10 days. Once this beachhead had been established, the Air Flotilla was moved ashore.

Aerial operations began on 23 October. This flight was vital for the Italians, as they hoped to keep an eye on the troop movements of the counteracting Turkish Army. Flying Nieuport Scouts (along with Farmans, Taubes, and Blériots) the Air Flotilla proved the value of timely aerial reconnaissance. Lasting approximately one year, the war ended with Tripoli becoming an Italian colony. More importantly, the military significance of aviation had been proven. No longer would warfare be restricted to frontline action.

Flight Setup.
Europe 1917—On.
Only the Airspeed Indicator and the Altimeter may be used on the Nieuport Scout.

Flight Objectives. Fly a reconnaissance mission.

Filing the Flight Plan.
Step 1. Take off from the main field.
Step 2. Keep the throttle setting below 1500 rpm.
Step 3. Fly the length of the boundary river at an altitude of 650 feet.
Step 4. Use a Downward View for watching the river as you fly.
Step 5. Return to the aerodrome and land.

Flight Debriefing. You will have successfully completed this flight if you:

☐ Examined the entire length of the river.
☐ Safely completed the flight.

7. PURSUING PANCHO VILLA

A troubled border separated Mexico and the United States at the turn of the century. Alternating its political stature in Mexico during a series of Mexican governmental changes, the United States fell into disfavor with one of Mexico's leading revolutionary figures. Francisco "Pancho" Villa began an armed aggression along the U.S.—Mexico border as retribution for America's foreign policy. His largest attack, on 9 March 1916, lead to an American invasion of Mexico.

Led by General John J. Pershing, a 5000-man force was ordered to locate and capture the elusive Villa. Supporting this massive ground effort was the First Aero Squadron. A force of eight Curtiss JN-2 Jenny aircraft formed the backbone of this aerial reconnaissance group. Aircraft losses, poor operating conditions, and the lack of adequate support equipment reduced the effectiveness of the First Aero Squadron. Subsequently, the two remaining JN-2s were withdrawn from the campaign on 22 April, with Pershing halting his hopeless mission in early 1917.

Flight Setup.
Auto-coordination—Off.
Reality mode—On.
Surface wind: Knots—8. Degrees—0.
Only the Airspeed Indicator and the Altimeter may be used on the Curtiss JN-2.
Flight Objectives. Fly a reconnaissance mission looking for Villa.
Filing the Flight Plan.
Step 1. Take off from San Antonio; 12083N 12578E Alt.—810.
Step 2. Keep the throttle setting below 1500 rpm.
Step 3. Fly a route to Laredo, Texas (11263N 12098E Alt.—508) at an altitude of 500 feet.
Step 4. Use a Downward View for watching the terrain as you fly.
Step 5. Return to San Antonio and land.
Flight Debriefing. You will have successfully completed this flight if you:

☐ Examined the area between San Antonio and Laredo.
☐ Safely completed the flight. This will be the hardest part of this flight. During the real hunt for Villa, eight Jennys started, but only two remained flyable at the conclusion of the campaign.

8. 5 OCTOBER 1914

On Sunday, 28 June 1914, a large crowd was gathering in Sarajevo, Bosnia, to greet the royal couple, Archduke Francis Ferdinand and his wife Sophie. As the royal motorcade made its appearance, Gavrilo Princip leapt onto the running board of Ferdinand's automobile and fired two shots from a pistol. Both the Archduke and his wife were killed. In just a few short months, the world would be plunged into one of its bloodiest wars.

As the battle lines were drawn, aerial reconnaissance played a vital role in determining the enemy's strengths and weaknesses. For the most part, fellow aviators paid little attention to the enemy's aircraft. Many pilots tried to achieve a tactical advantage by carrying weapons aloft in an attempt to shoot down the enemy's reconnaissance aircraft. Machine gun bullets quickly replaced friendly waves when the French pilots Frantz and Quénault shot down a German Aviatik with an armed Voisin.

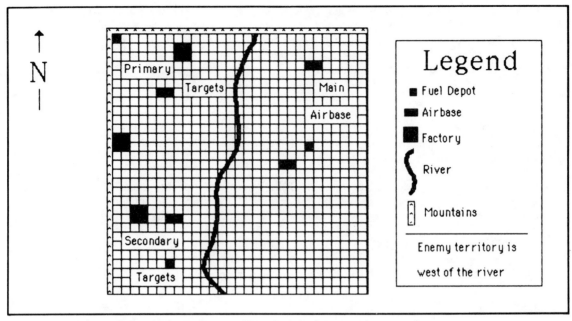

Fig. 6-1. This "recon photograph" will prove useful in all of the future combat scenarios.

Flight Setup.
Europe 1917—On.
Only the Airspeed Indicator and the Altimeter may be used on the Aviatik.
Flight Objectives. Fly a reconnaissance mission (Fig. 6-1).
Filing the Flight Plan.
Step 1. Declare war by pressing the W key (or Shift + W). Take off from the main field.
Step 2. Keep the throttle setting below 1500 rpm. Fire off all of your ammunition. You will not be using your machine guns during this flight.
Step 3. Fly to the enemy's primary airfield at an altitude of 800 feet. You are an unarmed aircraft.
Step 4. Use a Downward View for watching the airfield as you fly over.
Step 5. Return to the aerodrome and land.
Flight Debriefing. You will have successfully completed this flight if you:

☐ Examined the correct airfield.
☐ Safely completed the flight. Remember, the enemy fighters are armed and you are not.

9. 1 APRIL 1915

The early attempts at aerial combat usually involved awkward machine gun mountings, which offered the pilot a notoriously poor shooting platform. In an attempt to counteract the inaccuracy of this firing arrangement, R. Saulnier of the French Morane-Saulnier aircraft firm developed a method that allowed the pilot to mount a machine gun directly in front of his forward cockpit view. This mounting technique would naturally have destroyed the aircraft's propeller whenever the gun was fired. Saulnier, however, reinforced the propeller/bullet point of impact with steel deflector plates. Therefore, the machine gun could be fired at its natural pace without the fear of severing the propeller. As proof of the bullet deflector's validity, the French pilot Roland Garros scored the first aerial kill on 1 April 1915 in a Morane-Saulnier N that was armed with the Saulnier deflector plate scheme.

Flight Setup.

Europe 1917—On.

Only the Airspeed Indicator and the Altimeter may be used on the Morane-Saulnier N.

Flight Objectives. Match Roland Garros' kill.

Filing the Flight Plan.

Step 1. Declare war by pressing the W key (or Shift + W). Take off from the main field.

Step 2. Keep the throttle setting below 1500 rpm. Fire off 50 rounds of your ammunition.

Step 3. Fly to the enemy's primary airfield at an altitude of 800 feet. Engage any enemy aircraft that meet you.

Step 4. Shoot down one enemy fighter.

Step 5. Return to the aerodrome and land.

Flight Debriefing. You will have successfully completed this flight if you:

☐ Destroyed one enemy fighter.

☐ Safely completed the flight.

10. IMMELMANN

While the French continued their adoption of the steel deflector plate method of machine gun firing, the Germans developed a different method for shooting through the propeller's arc. By mounting an interrupter gear on the engine itself, the firing of a machine gun could be halted during those moments when the propeller blade was in the path of the bullet's flight. This far more efficient firing mechanism was first used on the Fokker E-I (many historians argue that Franz Schneider, instead of Anthony Fokker, should be credited with the invention of the interrupter gear).

Many German aces began their hunting careers in the Fokker E-I. One of the more brilliant of Germany's new-found aces was Max Immelmann. Known as the Eagle of Lille, Immelmann perfected aerial maneuvers, as well as his marksmanship. On 18 June 1916 Immelmann was killed in a dogfight near Lens. He had 15 kills at the time of his death.

Flight Setup.

Europe 1917—On.

Only the Airspeed Indicator and the Altimeter may be used on the Fokker E-I.

Flight Objectives. Score one kill.

Filing the Flight Plan.

Step 1. Declare war by pressing the W key (or Shift + W). Take off from the main field.

Step 2. Keep the throttle setting below 1500 rpm. Fire off 25 rounds of your ammunition.

Step 3. Fly to the enemy's primary airfield at an altitude of 800 feet. Engage any enemy aircraft that meet you. Rely on these three dogfighting techniques during this engagement: A. Have superior altitude. B. Always keep the enemy in front of you. C. Break off the combat when you have the advantage.

Step 4. Shoot down one enemy fighter.

Step 5. Return to the aerodrome and land.

Flight Debriefing. You will have successfully completed this flight if you:

☐ Destroyed one enemy fighter.

☐ Made Max Immelmann proud of your aerial skills.

☐ Safely completed the flight.

11. BATTLE OF VERDUN

World War I slowly evolved into a stagnant battle between entrenched foes. On 21 February 1916, Germany launched a major assault at disrupting this static front. Crown Prince Frederick Wilhelm concentrated his forces near the French town of Verdun. Following a 24-hour artillery barrage,

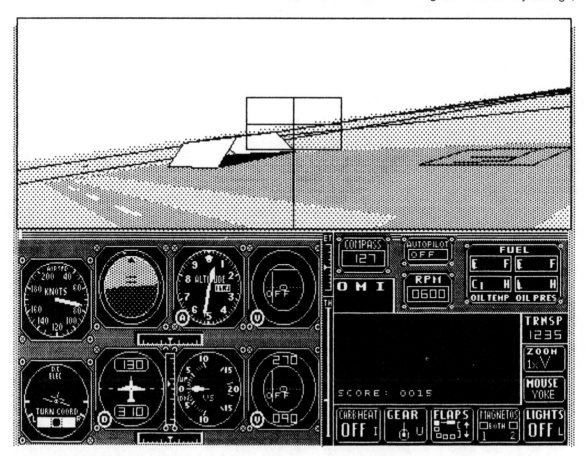

Fig. 6-2. Heavy enemy fighter activity has placed your D.H. 2 in serious jeopardy.

the Germans launched their attack along a 20-mile front. The French defense was solid and the Battle of Verdun dragged on for five months. Inflicting 540,000 casualties among the French forces and costing them a loss of 430,000 men, the Germans had advanced their line a meager four miles.

A strong reconnaissance air arm helped the French endure the constant German attacks. Armed scout aircraft such as the British Airco D.H. 2 helped maintain a watchful eye over German ground movements.

Flight Setup.

Europe 1917—On.

Only the Airspeed Indicator and the Altimeter may be used on the Airco D.H. 2.

Flight Objectives. Perform an armed reconnaissance.

Filing the Flight Plan.

Step 1. Declare war by pressing the W key (or Shift + W). Take off from the main field.

Step 2. Keep the throttle setting below 1500 rpm.

Step 3. Fly to the enemy's primary airfield at an altitude of 1000 feet. Avoid any armed conflicts.

Step 4. Use a Downward View for "photographing" the enemy base. If pressed into combat, use defensive maneuvers and shoot at the enemy fighters.

Step 5. Return to the aerodrome and land (Fig. 6-2).

Flight Debriefing. You will have successfully completed this flight if you:

☐ Delivered the recon film back to the home base.
☐ Safely completed the flight.

12. VON RICHTHOFEN

As the war dragged on, the pilots on both sides of the conflict became more proficient at staying alive in the air. Threatening a pilot's survival was an elite group of aviators that had achieved the status of ace. Among all of the aces from World War I, Germany's Manfred von Richthofen was ranked as the overall leader with a total of 80 confirmed kills.

Oddly enough, becoming a skilled hunter didn't exclude a pilot from himself being hunted. By flying a scarlet Fokker Dr.-I triplane (an aircraft with three parallel wings), von Richthofen had earned the nickname "Red Baron," along with the wrath of every Allied flier. On 21 April 1918, Canadian Captain A. R. Brown with No. 209 Squadron claimed the aerial kill of von Richthofen's Fokker. As a tribute to von Richthofen's superior flying skills, the British provided a full military burial for their fallen enemy.

Flight Setup.

Europe 1917—On.

Only the Airspeed Indicator and the Altimeter may be used on the Fokker Dr.-I.

Flight Objectives. Earn von Richthofen's 80th kill.

Filing the Flight Plan.

Step 1. Declare war by pressing the W key (or Shift + W). Take off from the main field.

Step 2. Keep the throttle setting below 1550 rpm.

Step 3. Fly to the enemy's primary airfield at an altitude of 1000 feet. Engage the enemy aircraft.

Step 4. Shoot down a single enemy fighter.

Step 5. Return to the aerodrome and land.

Flight Debriefing. You will have successfully completed this flight if you:

☐ Scored the Red Baron's 80th kill.

☐ Safely completed the flight. Following his last kill, von Richthofen is said to have passed low over the crashed pilot and waved a friendly greeting.

13. 24 MARCH 1918

In the trench warfare along the Western Front, deception was a key element in the success of an offensive. But beneath the constantly probing eyes of reconnaissance aircraft, troop movements could rarely be kept secret for very long. One method of limiting the effect of widespread reconnaissance flights was to fill the air with superior numbers of fighter aircraft. These huge fighter formations were usually met by an equally large force of escort fighters, which flew top cover for the recon aircraft.

Therefore, aerial combat between flights of 50 or more fighters became commonplace during 1918. During one of these enormous aerial conflicts, Captain J. L. Trollope of No. 43 Squadron set a new aerial record with six German kills on one sortie.

Flight Setup.

Europe 1917—On.

Only the Airspeed Indicator and the Altimeter may be used on the Sopwith Camel.

Flight Objectives. Score six aerial kills on one sortie.

Filing the Flight Plan.

Step 1. Declare war by pressing the W key (or Shift + W). Take off from the main field.

Step 2. Keep the throttle setting below 1600 rpm.

Step 3. Fly to the enemy's primary airfield at an altitude of 900 feet. Engage the enemy aircraft.

Step 4. Shoot down six enemy fighters.

Step 5. Return to the aerodrome and land.

Flight Debriefing. You will have successfully completed this flight if you:

☐ Shot down six enemy aircraft.

☐ Safely completed the flight. Less than one month after Trollope established his record, Captain H. W. Woollett duplicated the feat by downing six German flying machines on one sortie.

14. THE BIG PUSH

Determined to finally force an end to the carnage in Europe, Britain started a massive offensive, the Big Push, on 18 August 1918. Supported by numerous fighter and bomber squadrons, the combined Allied armies began to push Germany back towards its borders. Only through the complete domination of the skies was the Big Push able to succeed.

In the case of the Allies, air superiority came from numbers and not technology. Remarkable advances in aircraft technology increased the importance of air superiority over the battlefield. Most of these advanced aircraft failed to reach operational status prior to the signing of the Armistice, however. An example of an advanced Allied aircraft was the RAF's (Royal Air Force) Sopwith Snipe. Only a few test squadrons received this aircraft on a strictly evaluation basis.

Major W. G. Barker of No. 201 Squadron was able to put his Sopwith Snipe to the ultimate test when he was jumped by 15 German aircraft on 27 October 1918. Barker was able to shoot down four of the attacking enemy before he crash-landed behind British lines.

Flight Setup.

Europe 1917—On.

Only the Airspeed Indicator and the Altimeter may be used on the Sopwith Snipe.

Flight Objectives. Destroy four enemy aircraft.

Filing the Flight Plan.

Step 1. Declare war by pressing the W key (or Shift + W). Take off from the main field.

Step 2. Keep the throttle setting below 1750 rpm (Fig. 6-3).

Step 3. Fly to the enemy's secondary airfield at an altitude of 3000 feet. Engage the enemy aircraft.

Step 4. Shoot down four enemy fighters.

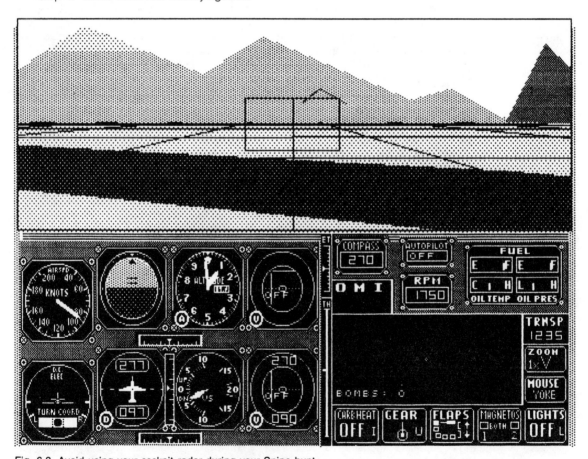

Fig. 6-3. Avoid using your cockpit radar during your Snipe hunt.

Step 5. Return to the aerodrome and land.

Flight Debriefing. You will have successfully completed this flight if you:

- ☐ Shot down four enemy aircraft.
- ☐ Safely completed the flight. Major Barker received extensive wounds during this engagement, not to mention the loss of his Sopwith Snipe. He was also awarded the Victoria Cross for his remarkable aerial feat.

15. TARGET OBENDORF

Aerial bombing was less than strategic from the biplanes and Zeppelins of either the Allied or the German Air Forces. Numerous raids were executed by both sides with only limited positive results. More often than not, the raiding force suffered greater casualties than the intended target. Britain's RNAS (Royal Naval Air Service) 3rd Wing became a portent of the type of true strategic bombing that would flatten Europe in less than 30 years. Flying nine Sopwith 1 1/2-Strutters and six French Breguet bombers, 3rd Wing carried out a successful bombing of the German Mauser factory at Obendorf on 12 October 1916. Although the amount of damage was lessened by the poor accuracy of the bombers, the seeds had been sown for long-range bombing in the next World War.

Flight Setup.

Europe 1917—On.

Only the Airspeed Indicator and the Altimeter may be used on the Breguet bomber.

Flight Objectives. Bomb the Mauser factory at Obendorf.

Filing the Flight Plan.

Step 1. Declare war by pressing the W key (or Shift + W). Take off from the main field.

Step 2. Keep the throttle setting below 1500 rpm. Jettison four of your five bombs over the river. Press the X key (or Shift + X) to drop each bomb.

Step 3. Fly to the enemy's primary factory at an altitude of 2000 feet.

Step 4. Bomb the factory.

Step 5. Return to the aerodrome and land.

Flight Debriefing. You will have successfully completed this flight if you:

- ☐ Bombed the Mauser factory. The actual raid by 3rd Wing yielded only a single bomb hit from the 15 aircraft that participated in the mission.
- ☐ Safely completed the flight.

Chapter 7

Barnstormer

16. SPEED RECORD 1923

First Lieutenant Russell L. Maughan established a new speed record of 205.455 knots while flying a Curtiss R-6 on 29 March 1923.

Flight Setup.

Auto-coordination—Off.

Reality mode—On.

Time: Hours—9. Minutes—00.

Season—Spring.

Surface wind: Knots—3. Degrees—275.

Reliability factor—90.

Only the Airspeed Indicator and the Altimeter may be used on the Curtiss R-6.

Flight Objectives. Break the 1923 speed record.

Filing the Flight Plan.

Step 1. Start the engine.

Step 2. Full engine rpm may be used.

Step 3. Take off from Dayton, Ohio; use 17417N 7446E Alt.—416 as a substitute for Dayton. Stay below an altitude of 328 feet.

Step 4. Assume straight and level flight. You must fly faster than 205 knots. Hold this speed for one minute.

Step 5. Return to the runway and land.

Step 6. Taxi to the airport's fueling location.

Flight Debriefing. You will have successfully completed this flight if you:

☐ Broke the 1923 speed record.

☐ Safely completed the flight.

17. MAIL RUN

Following the Great War, aviation was applied to more domestic chores. An ideal application for exploiting the speed advantage found in aircraft was in the delivery of perishable or time-sensitive materials. Commodities, such as the mail, could be loaded into an aircraft and flown directly to their destination in less time than the fastest ground transportation.

Understanding the value of quick mail delivery, Western Air Services, Inc., began its daily mail service between Los Angeles, California, and Salt Lake City, Utah, on 17 April 1926. Only the rugged and dependable Douglas M-2 was capable of flying the 660-mile distance with 1000 pounds of mail in under seven hours.

Flight Setup.
Auto-coordination—Off.
Reality mode—On.
Time: Hours—8. Minutes—00.
Season—Spring.
Cloud layer 1 tops—3000.
Cloud layer 1 bottoms—2500.
Surface wind: Knots—11. Degrees—180.
Reliability factor—70.
Only the Airspeed Indicator, Altimeter, and Compass may be used on the Douglas M-2.
Flight Objectives. Make the Western Air Service, Inc., mail run between LA and Salt Lake City.
Filing the Flight Plan.
Step 1. Start the engine. Fix the throttle at 1750 rpm.
Step 2. Take off from Los Angeles International Airport; 15379N 5811E Alt.—125. (You may want to use the slewing controls for moving across the country.)
Step 3. Land at Salt Lake City International Airport; 17648N 8719E Alt.—4228.
Flight Debriefing. You will have successfully completed this flight if you:

☐ Delivered the mail.
☐ Flew from LA to Salt Lake City.
☐ Safely completed the journey. An exact duplication of the Western Air Service route made a stop in Las Vegas, Nevada.

18. STUNT RIDE—$25

Shortly after the cessation of hostilities in Europe, many of the Air Service pilots were demobilized. Therefore, in 1919 and 1920 many young men and women who knew only one skill—flying—were out of work. In an attempt to regain the splendor of their former glory, a unique cadre of discharged military aviators toured America's heartland and provided local residents with a chance to witness the marvels of flight. Known as barnstormers, these pilots flew with very little supervision and a minimum of supplies. In spite of these limitations, an entire future generation of aviators received their first aerial encounter at the hands of the barnstormer.

Flight Setup.
Auto-coordination—Off.
Reality mode—On.

Time: Hours—11. Minutes—30.
Season—Summer.
Surface wind: Knots—3. Degrees—160.
Reliability factor—50.
Only the Airspeed Indicator, Altimeter, and Compass may be used on the Curtiss JN-4 Jenny.
Flight Objectives. Give a $25 stunt ride.
Filing the Flight Plan.
Step 1. Start the engine. Fix the throttle at 1600 rpm.
Step 2. Take off from Buckeye, Arizona; 14610N 7679E Alt.—1023.
Step 3. Climb to an altitude of 2500 feet.
Step 4. Enter a shallow dive and execute a loop.
Step 5. Dive to an altitude of 500 feet. Make a sharp climbing pullout.
Step 6. Land back at Buckeye.
Flight Debriefing. You will have successfully completed this flight if you:

☐ Gave the passenger a stunt ride.
☐ Didn't lose the passenger somewhere over Buckeye.
☐ Safely completed the flight.

19. FLYING UNDER BRIDGES

As more and more military pilots entered the barnstorming tour circuit, the price for rides diminished rapidly. Gone were the days of $20 and $25 rides. By 1925, the price for a three-minute ride had plummeted to $3. Gradually, the barnstormer developed more daring flight escapades in an attempt to stymie this price drop. Flying around manmade obstacles was a natural "death-cheating" activity for these desperate pilots. Basically, if the local town had a large barn, then the barnstormer would fly through it. Or, if a bridge spanned a sizable body of water, then the barnstormer would fly under the bridge. Unfortunately, some of the pilots were unable to cheat death with these activities.

Flight Setup.
Auto-coordination—Off.
Reality mode—On.
Time: Hours—14. Minutes—00.
Season—Summer.
Surface wind: Knots—3. Degrees—160.
Reliability factor—50.
Only the Airspeed Indicator, Altimeter, and Compass may be used on the Curtiss JN-4 Jenny.
Flight Objectives. Fly under the Golden Gate Bridge.
Filing the Flight Plan.
Step 1. Start the engine. Fix the throttle at 1600 rpm.
Step 2. Take off from Hamilton Army Field in San Francisco, CA; 17534N 5082E Alt.—3.
(Use the San Francisco and The Bay Area Star Scenery Disk for the greatest visual effect.)
Step 3. Climb to an altitude of 500 feet.
Step 4. Locate the Golden Gate Bridge.
Step 5. Fly under the bridge.

Step 6. Return to Hamilton Army Field and land.

Flight Debriefing. You will have successfully completed this flight if you:

☐ Flew under the Golden Gate Bridge.
☐ Safely completed the flight. If you *really* feel like cheating death, attempt to do a loop around the Golden Gate Bridge.

20. LOOP-THE-LOOP

In addition to flying dangerously close to, in, and around manmade landmarks, the barnstormer also made a habit of performing difficult aerial maneuvers with great abandon. A perennial favorite among the county fair crowd was a series of repetitive consecutive loops. Every barnstormer who tried to satisfy the customer's demands for this particular maneuver suffered from constant maintenance problems—not to mention the life-threatening aspects of such careless flight.

Flight Setup.
Auto-coordination—Off.
Reality mode—On.
Time: Hours—15. Minutes—30.
Season—Summer.
Cloud layer 1 tops—5000.
Cloud layer 1 bottoms—3000.
Surface wind: Knots—1. Degrees—80.
Reliability factor—50.
Only the Airspeed Indicator, Altimeter, and Compass may be used on the Curtiss JN-4 Jenny.

Flight Objectives. Perform 10 consecutive loops.

Filing the Flight Plan.
Step 1. Start the engine. Fix the throttle at 1600 rpm.
Step 2. Take off from Van Nuys, California; 15488N 5816E Alt.—800.
Step 3. Climb to an altitude of 3100 feet.
Step 4. Execute 10 consecutive loops.
Step 5. Return to Van Nuys and land.

Flight Debriefing. You will have successfully completed this flight if you:

☐ Completed 10 consecutive loops.
☐ Safely completed the flight.

21. TOPEKA, KS

If nothing else, the barnstormer brought the excitement of flight to areas where the airplane was still a mystery. To this end, the Midwest became the most frequented tour area for the barnstormer. Interestingly enough, many of the towns and cities that were visited by these pilots would later become thriving centers for the aviation industry.

Flight Setup.

Auto-coordination—Off.

Reality mode—On.

Time: Hours—10. Minutes—00.

Season—Summer.

Surface wind: Knots—9. Degrees—270.

Reliability factor—50.

Only the Airspeed Indicator, Altimeter, and Compass may be used on the Curtiss JN-4 Jenny.

Flight Objectives. Give an aerial demonstration over Topeka, KS.

Filing the Flight Plan.

Step 1. Start the engine. Fix the throttle at 1600 rpm.

Step 2. Take off from Forbes Field in Topeka, KS; 15957N 13899E Alt.—1079.

Step 3. Climb to an altitude of 3000 feet.

Step 4. Perform two consecutive loops.

Step 5. Climb back to 3000 feet and stall the aircraft.

Step 6. Recover from the stall at 1500 feet.

Step 7. Make a high-speed pass down the middle of runway 3.

Step 8. Return to Forbes Field and land.

Flight Debriefing. You will have successfully completed this flight if you:

☐ Completed the required maneuvers.

☐ Safely completed the flight.

22. CHICAGO, IL

There were three standout cities where a typical barnstormer could gain the maximum profit from her or his craft: Chicago, Illinois; Omaha, Nebraska; and Wichita, Kansas. Each of these cities offered a special attraction. For example, in Chicago a regular series of air races, along with the Chicago Aircraft Show, fostered an aviation atmosphere rich with sophisticated audiences that appreciated talented pilots.

Flight Setup.

Auto-coordination—Off.

Reality mode—On.

Time: Hours—8. Minutes—35.

Season—Summer.

Cloud layer 1 tops—5000.

Cloud layer 1 bottoms—4000.

Wind level 1: Knots—415. Degrees—40.

Surface wind: Knots—11. Degrees—300.

Reliability factor—50.

Only the Airspeed Indicator, Altimeter, and Compass may be used on the Curtiss JN-4 Jenny.

Flight Objectives. Give an aerial demonstration over Chicago, IL.

Filing the Flight Plan.

Step 1. Start the engine. Fix the throttle at 1600 rpm.

Step 2. Take off from Meigs Field in Chicago, IL; 17189N 16671E Alt.—592.

Step 3. Climb to an altitude of 4000 feet.

Step 4. Perform four consecutive loops.

Step 5. Climb back to 2000 feet.

Step 6. Cut the engine and dive to 1000 feet.

Step 7. Restart the engine and climb back to 1500 feet.

Step 8. Return to Meigs Field and land.

Flight Debriefing. You will have successfully completed this flight if you:

☐ Completed the required maneuvers.

☐ Safely completed the flight.

23. OMAHA, NE

Two features were predominant in Omaha, Nebraska's attraction to the barnstormer. First and foremost was the presence of money. Omaha was (and still is) a major cattle and grain market in the Great Plains. Lending further support to the financial benefits of this area was a strong influence from the Union Pacific Railroad. The second attribute of Omaha was its central positioning for supplying the cross-country traveling barnstormer. It was not uncommon to see a famous pilot, such as Charles Holman (see Flight Scenario 25) finding time to thrill Omaha crowds as part of his nomadic flying life.

Flight Setup.

Auto-coordination—Off.

Reality mode—On.

Time: Hours—9. Minutes—45.

Season—Summer.

Cloud layer 1 tops—4500.

Cloud layer 1 bottoms—3000.

Surface wind: Knots—5. Degrees—320.

Reliability factor—50.

Only the Airspeed Indicator, Altimeter, and Compass may be used on the Curtiss JN-4 Jenny.

Flight Objectives. Give an aerial demonstration over Omaha, NE.

Filing the Flight Plan.

Step 1. Start the engine. Fix the throttle at 1600 rpm.

Step 2. Take off from Eppley Airfield in Omaha, NE; 17060N 13902E Alt.—984.

Step 3. Climb to an altitude of 3200 feet.

Step 4. Perform three consecutive loops.

Step 5. Climb back to 2000 feet.

Step 6. Perform two consecutive loops.

Step 7. Stall the aircraft at 3500 feet and recover at 1000 feet.

Step 8. Return to Eppley Airfield and land.

Flight Debriefing. You will have successfully completed this flight if you:

☐ Completed the required maneuvers.

☐ Safely completed the flight.

24. WICHITA, KS

Wichita, Kansas' claim to barnstormer fame was the presence of such legendary aviation names as Laird, Burke, Moellendick, and Witt. Guiding companies such as Wichita Aircraft Company and E. M. Laird Company, these four men shaped the future of civilian aviation's premier city. Eventually, the more familiar names began to appear in Wichita—Stearman, Beech, and Cessna— and Wichita became the capital of the civilian aircraft industry.

Flight Setup.
Auto-coordination—Off.
Reality mode—On.
Time: Hours—10. Minutes—00.
Season—Summer.
Surface wind: Knots—21. Degrees—10.
Reliability factor—50.
Only the Airspeed Indicator, Altimeter, and Compass may be used on the Curtiss JN-4 Jenny.
Flight Objectives. Give an aerial demonstration over Wichita, KS.
Filing the Flight Plan.
Step 1. Start the engine. Fix the throttle at 1600 rpm.
Step 2. Take off from Wichita, KS; 15460N 13250E Alt.—1332.
Step 3. Climb to an altitude of 3600 feet.
Step 4. Perform five consecutive loops.
Step 5. Climb back to 4000 feet with a 90 degree up pitch.
Step 6. Just before the aircraft stalls, turn earthward by using only the rudder. Use hard right rudder. Neutralize the rudder when the aircraft's nose is pointed home. (This is a hammerhead turn.)
Step 7. Recover from the hammerhead turn at 1500 feet.
Step 8. Return to the Wichita Airport and land.
Flight Debriefing. You will have successfully completed this flight if you:

☐ Completed the required maneuvers.
☐ Safely completed the flight.

25. SPEED HOLMAN

The days of the barnstormer waned in the late 1920s and early 1930s. Very few people were willing to pay even $3 for a circuitous flight around their local airfield when they could purchase an airline ticket for under $100. Indeed, the pilots themselves were engaged in more serious and profitable ventures. Aircraft racing provided the aviator with the excitement of competition flying and the financial security of a large company's backing.

Seeking the fame and fortune afforded the racing pilot, Charles "Speed" Holman turned from his barnstorming roots to aviation racing. Holman's first major victory was the New York-to-Spokane Class A Race of 1927 in the cockpit of a Laird Speedwing. His greatest victory was in winning the 1930 Thompson Trophy Race in a Laird Solution at an average speed of 201.9 mph. An ominous after effect of this race was Holman's being poisoned by the exhaust from the Laird Solution. Charles Holman was also able to combine his racing interests with a rewarding "day" job as a pilot for Northwest Airways.

Flight Setup.

Auto-coordination—Off.

Reality mode—On.

Time: Hours—18. Minutes—30.

Season—Spring.

Surface wind: Knots—7. Degrees—140.

Reliability factor—50.

Only the Airspeed Indicator, Altimeter, and Compass may be used on the Laird Speedwing.

Flight Objectives. Fly Speed Holman's last flight.

Filing the Flight Plan.

Step 1. Start the engine. Fix the throttle at 1600 rpm.

Step 2. Take off from Eppley Airfield in Omaha, NE; 17060N 13902E Alt.—984.

Step 3. Climb to an altitude of 3000 feet.

Step 4. Perform a loop.

Step 5. Climb back to 1000 feet.

Step 6. Line up on runway 14 R. Use only the ailerons to roll the aircraft into an inverted attitude.

Step 7. Lower your altitude until you are 50 feet above the ground.

Step 8. At the end of the runway, pitch the nose of the aircraft up. (Remember to use *down* elevator for this maneuver during inverted flight.)

Step 9. Return to Eppley Airfield and land.

Flight Debriefing. You will have successfully completed this flight if you:

☐ Completed the required maneuvers.

☐ Safely completed the flight. If you are able to meet this requirement, then you flew this scenario better than Speed Holman. According to eyewitness accounts, Holman lost control of his Laird Speedwing while in inverted flight. Pitching the nose of his aircraft down, instead of up, caused the Laird Speedwing to crash near Eppley Airfield in Omaha, Nebraska, on 17 May 1931.

Chapter 8

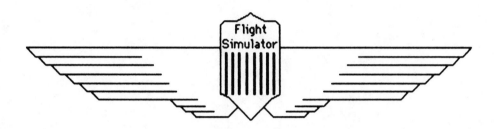

Seat of Your Pants

26. ROUND-THE-WORLD IN 175 DAYS

After 21 years of service, the true value of the airplane came under question in 1924. What beneficial impact on humanity did aircraft have to offer? Fast, efficient transportation became the obvious test of the airplane's validity. In an effort to prove the airplane's superior capabilities at prolonged travel, the U.S. Army Air Service proposed a round-the-world flight for the spring and summer months of 1924. Organized into a flight of four Douglas World Cruisers, named *Seattle, Chicago, Boston,* and *New Orleans,* the world tour began on 6 April 1924 from Seattle, Washington. With stops in Alaska, Japan, China, India, Persia, the Balkans, France, and Nova Scotia, only two of the original aircraft were able to complete the entire journey back to Seattle, arriving on 28 September 1924.

Flight Setup.
Auto-coordination—Off.
Reality mode—On.
Time: Hours—13. Minutes—00.
Season—Summer.
Cloud layer 1 tops—8500.
Cloud layer 1 bottoms—5500.
Surface wind: Knots—9. Degrees—320.
Reliability factor—80.

Only the Airspeed Indicator, Altimeter, Compass, and Artificial Horizon may be used on the Douglas World Cruiser. (The actual aircraft only had a compass, an altimeter, and an artificial horizon.)

Flight Objectives. Follow the path of the *Chicago* through Japan.

Filing the Flight Plan.
Step 1. Start the engine. Fix the throttle at 1600 rpm.
Step 2. Take off from Osaka International Airport; 17267N 31528E Alt.—49. (Use the Japan

Scenery Disk for this scenario.)

    Step 3. Climb to an altitude of 10,000 feet.

    Step 4. Fly towards Tokyo International Airport; 18201N 32787E Alt.—12.

    Step 5. Drop below the cloud cover as you near Yokohama.

    Step 6. Land on runway 22 at Tokyo International.

    Flight Debriefing. You will have successfully completed this flight if you:

☐ Followed the specified course.

☐ Safely completed the flight.

27. FLYING BLIND

Significant strides began reaching the aviation industry in the 1920s. Aside from the airframe and powerplant improvements, aircraft instrumentation proved essential in making the airplane fit for all seasons. Several skeptics, however, shared the opinion that instruments, no matter how extensive and elaborate, could never replace the eyes of a human being staring out from a cockpit.

It fell to Lt. Jimmy Doolittle to prove this belief wrong. On 24 September 1929, Lt. Doolittle isolated himself inside the cockpit of a Consolidated NY-2 and piloted a 15-minute flight around Mitchel Field, Long Island.

Flight Setup.

Auto-coordination—Off.

Reality mode—On.

Time: Hours—22. Minutes—30.

Season—Fall.

Surface wind: Knots—305. (This is a turbulence factor of 3 and a wind speed of 5 knots.) Degrees—40.

Reliability factor—90.

Only the Airspeed Indicator, Altimeter, Compass, and Artificial Horizon may be used on the Consolidated NY-2.

Flight Objectives. Use only the aircraft's instruments for flying a short 15-minute flight.

Filing the Flight Plan.

Step 1. Start the engine. Fix the throttle at 1750 rpm. Use a Downward View so that you won't be tempted to "look" out the front of the cockpit. Turn on the interior lights.

Step 2. Take off from John F. Kennedy International Airport; 17034N 21065E Alt.—12.

Step 3. Climb to an altitude of 2000 feet.

Step 4. Execute a right bank.

Step 5. Make a visual sighting of Kennedy International. Switch back to a Forward View for this temporary sighting.

Step 6. Line up on runway 22 R at John F. Kennedy International Airport.

Flight Debriefing. You will have successfully completed this flight if you:

☐ Flew the specified maneuvers using instruments only.

☐ Safely completed the flight.

28. KNIGHT INTO DAY

Air mail delivery fought a hard battle for a right to exist in the early 1920s. Crashes, poor maintenance, and inclement weather convinced Congress that the fledgling air mail branch of the Post Office should be terminated. In a desperate attempt to save the air mail service, Postmaster General Albert Burleson created one last demonstration of the viability of this speedy letter delivery system.

Four deHavilland DH-4s were assigned to fly two crossing routes from the east-to-west coast and from the west-to-east coast. Starting on 22 February 1921, the two DH-4s leaving from New York were halted at Chicago, Illinois, by a winter storm. Meanwhile, one of the two DH-4s leaving from San Francisco crashed in Nevada. This left only one of the four mail planes able to make the cross-country attempt. Unfortunately, a blizzard was standing between the mail plane and a successful completion of the air mail delivery.

The pilot who took over the DH-4 in North Platte, Nebraska, was James H. Knight. Determined not to let the air mail branch of the post office fail, Knight flew the loaded DH-4 from North Platte to Omaha, Nebraska, at 1950 hours. Refueled, he continued on to Iowa City, Iowa. After one final refueling, Knight landed at Checkerboard Field in Chicago at 0840 hours. Once in Chicago, two other pilots flew the DH-4 the remainder of its leg into New York. Knight's effort so impressed President Harding that Congress voted to continue the air mail service.

Flight Setup.
Auto-coordination—Off.
Reality mode—On.
Time: Hours—19. Minutes—50.
Season—Winter.
Cloud layer 1 tops—10,000.
Cloud layer 1 bottoms—3500.
Surface wind: Knots—635. Degrees—40.
Reliability factor—95.
Only the Airspeed Indicator, Altimeter, Compass, and Artificial Horizon may be used on the deHavilland DH-4.

Flight Objectives. Fly the mail from North Platte, Nebraska to Chicago, Illinois.
Filing the Flight Plan.
Step 1. Start the engine. Fix the throttle at 1750 rpm.
Step 2. Take off from Lee Bird Field in North Platte, NE; 17086N 12332E Alt.—2778.
Step 3. Stay low to avoid any storm activity.
Step 4. Fly to Omaha, NE; 17060N 13902E Alt.—984. Refuel and take off.
Step 5. Fly to Des Moines, Iowa; 17150N 14625E Alt.—958. Refuel and take off again.
Step 6. Fly to Meigs Field in Chicago, IL; 17189N 16671E Alt.—592.
Step 7. Land on runway 18 at Meigs Field.
Flight Debriefing. You will have successfully completed this flight if you:

☐ Flew the specified route and made the correct number of stops.
☐ Delivered the mail in under 13 hours of flying time.
☐ Safely completed the flight.

29. SOLO WOMAN

On 20 May 1927, Charles Lindbergh proved that dramatic solo flight was possible by flying from New York to Paris, France. This feat opened up a floodgate of record-breaking attempts. Along with each milestone flight, a new hero was thrust into the public spotlight.

In striking contrast to the large number of male aviators was a small group of female fliers who were even more endearing to the news media. Chief among these diminutive daredevils was Amelia Earhart. Following a solo flight across the Atlantic on 20 May 1932, Earhart flew solo nonstop across the United States on 24 August 1932. Both of these record-breaking flights were made in Amelia's famous scarlet Lockheed 5B Vega.

Flight Setup.
Auto-coordination—Off.
Reality mode—On.
Time: Hours—6. Minutes—00.
Season—Summer.
Surface wind: Knots—205. Degrees—250.
Reliability factor—95.
Only the Airspeed Indicator, Altimeter, Compass, and Artificial Horizon may be used on the Lockheed 5B Vega.

Flight Objectives. Fly Amelia Earhart's solo transcontinental flight.

Filing the Flight Plan.
Step 1. Start the engine. Fix the throttle at 1900 rpm.
Step 2. Take off from Los Angeles International Airport; 15374N 5805E Alt.—126. (Use the slewing control for this scenario.)
Step 3. Fly to John F. Kennedy International Airport; 17034N 21065E Alt.—12.
Step 4. Land at Kennedy International Airport.

Flight Debriefing. You will have successfully completed this flight if you:

☐ Flew the specified route.
☐ Completed the flight in less than 20 hours of elapsed time.
☐ Safely completed the flight.

30. JETSTREAM *WINNIE MAE*

By the early 1930s, records for speed, altitude, and distance were being set and broken with regularity. Trying to establish a unique record that combined all three of these categories, Wiley Post modified the structure of his Lockheed 5C Vega, the *Winnie Mae*. Adding a supercharger and jettisonable landing gear, Post figured that he could reach extreme altitudes and place his aircraft in the jetstream. In turn, the strong currents in the jetstream would catapult the Vega along at a greater ground speed. Finally, in order for Post to be able to function in the limited atmosphere of these higher altitudes, B. F. Goodrich Company designed a special pilot pressure suit. The first test of this "new" *Winnie Mae* came on 15 March 1935, when Post flew from Burbank, California, to Cleveland, Ohio, in less than 7 1/2 hours.

Flight Setup.
Auto-coordination—Off.
Reality mode—On.

Time: Hours—8. Minutes—00.
Season—spring.
Cloud layer 1 tops—9500.
Cloud layer 1 bottoms—3000.
Wind level 1: Knots—60. Degrees—270.
Shear zone altitude—10,000.
Surface wind: Knots—35. Degrees—0.
Reliability factor—95.
Only the Airspeed Indicator, Altimeter, Compass, and Artificial Horizon may be used on the Lockheed 5C Vega.

Flight Objectives. Fly Wiley Post's high-speed, high-altitude record flight.

Filing the Flight Plan.

Step 1. Start the engine. Fix the throttle at 2200 rpm.

Step 2. Take off from Burbank, CA; 15478N 5861E Alt.—774. (Use the slewing control for this scenario.)

Step 3. Climb to an altitude of 10,000 feet.

Step 4. Fly to Cleveland, Ohio. (Use 17417N 7447E Alt.—416 to represent Cleveland.)

Step 5. Land at Cleveland, Ohio.

Flight Debriefing. You will have successfully completed this flight if you:

☐ Flew the specified route.
☐ Completed the flight in less than 8 hours of elapsed time.
☐ Safely completed the flight.

Chapter 9

Air Racing

31. INTERNATIONAL BENNETT CUP 1920

A tradition with international air races is that the country holding the award serves as host for the following year's race. Therefore, on 28 September 1920, Villesauvage Airdrome at Etampes, France, served as the site for the 1920 International Bennett Cup race. This year fielded six entrants—three from France, two from the United States, and one from Great Britain. Neither of the Americans—Howard Rinehart flying a Dayton-Wright RB-1 and Shorty Schroeder piloting a Verville-Packard R-1—were able to finish the race. France's Sadi-Lecointe in a Nieuport 29 won the race at an average speed of 146.4 knots.

Flight Setup.
Auto-coordination—Off.
Reality mode—On.
Time: Hours—8. Minutes—00.
Season—Fall.
Surface wind: Knots—404. Degrees—0.
Reliability factor—30.
Only the Airspeed Indicator, Altimeter, Compass, and Artificial Horizon may be used on the Dayton-Wright RB-1.
The landing gear may be retracted during this scenario.
Flight Objectives. See if you can win the International Bennett Cup in the Dayton-Wright RB-1.
Filing the Flight Plan.
Step 1. Start the engine. Full throttle may be used during this race.
Step 2. Take off from Villesauvage Airdrome; 17418N 7448E Alt.—410.
Step 3. Climb to an altitude of 1000 feet.
Step 4. Fly faster than 146.4 knots in a straight and level attitude.
Step 5. Turn around and duplicate this speed on a heading back to Villesauvage.
Step 6. Land at Villesauvage Airdrome.

Flight Debriefing. You will have successfully completed this flight if you:

☐ Flew faster than 146.4 knots.
☐ Safely completed the flight. During the race, Rinehart was forced to exit the competition when he broke a rudder cable on his Dayton-Wright RB-1.

32. PULITZER TROPHY RACE 1920

The Pulitzer Trophy Race of 1920 was the first major air race held in the United States for eight years. An international field of 37 aircraft entered the race, with only 25 of the entries being able to finish.

The race consisted of four laps around a 29.02 mile long course. Taking off from Mitchel Field, New York, on 27 November 1920, the 37 aircraft provided an exciting contest that wasn't decided until the last mile of the race. Captain Corliss Mosely flying a Verville-Packard R-1 won at an average speed of 136 knots.

Flight Setup.
Auto-coordination—Off.
Reality mode—On.
Time: Hours—8. Minutes—00.
Season—Fall.
Surface wind: Knots—624. Degrees—0.
Reliability factor—80.
Only the Airspeed Indicator, Altimeter, Compass, and Artificial Horizon may be used on the Verville-Packard R-1.

Flight Objectives. Win the Pulitzer Trophy Race of 1920.

Filing the Flight Plan.
Step 1. Start the engine. Full throttle may be used during this race.
Step 2. Take off from John F. Kennedy International Airport; 17034N 21065E Alt.—12.
Step 3. Climb to an altitude of 1000 feet.
Step 4. Fly faster than 136 knots in a straight and level attitude to Bridgeport, CT; 17287N 21249E Alt.—10.
Step 5. Turn around and duplicate this speed on a heading back to JFK.
Step 6. Land at New York's JFK.

Flight Debriefing. You will have successfully completed this flight if you:

☐ Flew faster than 136 knots.
☐ Safely completed the flight.

33. PULITZER TROPHY RACE 1921

Unlike international air races, domestic races were held at various sites around the country. In

1921, for example, the Pulitzer Trophy Race was held at Omaha, Nebraska. Six pilots entered the 155.35 mile race. On 3 November, 1921, Bert Acosta left the other five contestants behind as he flew his Curtiss CR-1 to a record course speed of 153.6 knots. Clarence Coombs finished a close second in a unique triplane, *Cactus Kitten* (just one year earlier, the *Cactus Kitten* had been a biplane), flying at approximately 148 knots.

Flight Setup.

Auto-coordination—Off.

Reality mode—On.

Time: Hours—8. Minutes—00.

Season—Fall.

Surface wind: Knots—30. Degrees—210.

Reliability factor—80.

Only the Airspeed Indicator, Altimeter, Compass, and Artificial Horizon may be used on the Curtiss CR-1.

Flight Objectives. Win the Pulitzer Trophy Race of 1921.

Filing the Flight Plan.

Step 1. Start the engine. Full throttle may be used during this race.

Step 2. Take off from Eppley Airfield in Omaha, NE; 17060N 13902E Alt.—984.

Step 3. Climb to an altitude of 1000 feet.

Step 4. Fly faster than 148 knots in a straight and level attitude to Lincoln, NE; 16876N 13608E Alt.—1214.

Step 5. Turn around and duplicate this speed on a heading back to Omaha.

Step 6. Land at Eppley Airfield.

Flight Debriefing. You will have successfully completed this flight if you:

☐ Flew faster than 148 knots.

☐ Safely completed the flight.

34. SCHNEIDER TROPHY RACE 1923

Air racing moved back overseas when Great Britain hosted the 1923 Schneider Trophy Race. In direct contrast with other races, the Schneider Trophy Race was held only for seaplanes. What began as a ten-aircraft race ended with only five aircraft beginning the race. On 28 September 1923, these five international entries started their 214.3 mile race from Cowes, England. Two float-equipped American Curtiss R-6s finished first and second in the race. David Rittenhouse piloted the winning R-6 to a speed in excess of 154.2 knots, with Rutledge Irvine flying his R-6 in second place at 150.8 knots.

Flight Setup.

Auto-coordination—Off.

Reality mode—On.

Time: Hours—8. Minutes—00.

Season—Fall.

Surface wind: Knots—37. Degrees—322.

Reliability factor—80.

Only the Airspeed Indicator, Altimeter, Compass, and Artificial Horizon may be used on the Curtiss R-6.

Flight Objectives. Win the Schneider Trophy Race of 1923.

Filing the Flight Plan.

Step 1. Start the engine. Full throttle may be used during this race.

Step 2. Take off from Cowes, England (we'll be using Moffett Naval Air Station instead); 17220N 5134E Alt.—34. (Use the San Francisco Area Star Scenery Disk for this scenario.)

Step 3. Climb to an altitude of 1000 feet.

Step 4. Fly faster than 154.2 knots in a straight and level attitude to Hamilton Army Field; 17534N 5082E Alt.—3.

Step 5. Turn around and duplicate this speed on a heading back to Moffett.

Step 6. Repeat this flight pattern one more time.

Step 7. Land at Moffett NAS.

Flight Debriefing. You will have successfully completed this flight if you:

☐ Flew faster than 154.2 knots.
☐ Safely completed the flight.

35. NATIONAL AIR RACE 1927

Several air races were organized that featured numerous racing activities throughout a week-long event. The National Air Race of 1927 lasted seven days in late September at Spokane, Washington. Along with the standard aerobatic exhibitions, there were two noteworthy races. The first was a New York-to-Spokane Class A race. This event was won by Speed Holman (see Flight Scenario 25). The second race was the Spokesman-Review Trophy Cup Race for military pursuit aircraft. A total of 10 Army and Navy aircraft entered this competition. The race was won by Army Air Corps Lt. Eugene Batten with a Curtiss XP-6A and a speed of 174.8 knots.

Flight Setup.

Auto-coordination—Off.

Reality mode—On.

Time: Hours—14. Minutes—30.

Season—Fall.

Cloud layer 1 tops—3000.

Cloud layer 1 bottoms—1200.

Surface wind: Knots—21. Degrees—120.

Reliability factor—80.

Only the Airspeed Indicator, Altimeter, Compass, and Artificial Horizon may be used on the Curtiss XP-6A.

Flight Objectives. Win the Spokesman-Review Trophy of 1927.

Filing the Flight Plan.

Step 1. Start the engine. Full throttle may be used during this race.

Step 2. Take off from Spokane International Airport; 20923N 7924E Alt.—2371.

Step 3. Climb to an altitude of 3000 feet.

Step 4. Fly faster than 174.8 knots in a straight and level attitude to Deer Park; 21051N 8004E Alt.—2207.

Step 5. Turn around and duplicate this speed on a heading back to Spokane.

Step 6. Land at Spokane International Airport.

Flight Debriefing. You will have successfully completed this flight if you:

☐ Flew faster than 174.8 knots.
☐ Safely completed the flight.

36. BENDIX TROPHY RACE 1933

As the airspeeds of the racers increased, long distance races, such as the Bendix Trophy Race, became more practical. Furthermore, female pilots were allowed to compete directly with other aviators in these cross-country events.

The finish of the Bendix Trophy Race of 1933 was used as an opening ceremony for the National Air Races, which began in Los Angeles, California on 1 July 1933. Six planes took off from the starting line in New York. The roster of entrants read like an aviation "Who's Who." Roscoe Turner was flying a Wedell-Williams Special. Jim Wedell also piloted a Wedell-Williams Special. Filling out the remainder of the field were two Gee Bee racers (the R-1 and the R-2) with Russell Boardman and Russell Thaw at the controls, along with another Wedell-Williams Special flown by Lee Gehlbach. Amelia Earhart filled the final entry spot with her famous Lockheed Vega.

Only two of these aircraft finished the race in LA. Gehlbach had engine trouble, Thaw crashed, Boardman was killed in a crash, and Earhart had a faulty engine. This left Roscoe Turner to win the Bendix Trophy with an average speed of 185.97 knots.

Flight Setup.
Auto-coordination—Off.
Reality mode—On.
Time: Hours—7. Minutes—00.
Season—Summer.
Cloud layer 1 tops—9000.
Cloud layer 1 bottoms—6000.
Surface wind: Knots—7. Degrees—180.
Reliability factor—80.
Only the Airspeed Indicator, Altimeter, Compass, and Artificial Horizon may be used on the Wedell-Williams Special.

Flight Objectives. Win the Bendix Trophy Race of 1933.

Filing the Flight Plan.
Step 1. Start the engine. Full throttle may be used during this race.
Step 2. Take off from John F. Kennedy International Airport; 17034N 21065E Alt.—12.
Step 3. Climb to an altitude of 8000 feet. (Use the slewing controls with this scenario.)
Step 4. Fly faster than 185.97 knots in a straight and level attitude to Los Angeles International Airport; 15374N 5805E Alt.—126.
Step 5. Land at LAX.

Flight Debriefing. You will have successfully completed this flight if you:

☐ Flew faster than 185.97 knots.
☐ Safely completed the flight.

37. THOMPSON TROPHY RACE 1933

By 1933, air racing was a dominant sport in the United States. In fact, date conflicts prevented many pilots from participating in the enormous number of races that were held each year. A case in point was the overlapping dates for the Thompson Trophy Race and the National Air Races. As such, the Thompson Trophy Race attracted only six entrants. Back again were Turner, Gehlback, and Wedell, all flying Wedell-Williams Specials. Additionally, Zantford Granville piloting a Gee Bee Model Y, Roy Minor with Ben Howard's *Mike,* and George Hague in Keith Rider's *Bumblebee* competed in the race. Roscoe Turner flew the fastest speed in the six-lap event, but he missed a pylon on the second lap and was disqualified. This left James Wedell as the winner of the Thompson Trophy Race with an average speed of 206.8 knots.

Flight Setup.
Auto-coordination—Off.
Reality mode—On.
Time: Hours—14. Minutes—00.
Season—Summer.
Surface wind: Knots—11. Degrees—90.
Reliability factor—80.

Only the Airspeed Indicator, Altimeter, Compass, and Artificial Horizon may be used on the Wedell-Williams Special.

Flight Objectives. Win the Thompson Trophy Race of 1933.

Filing the Flight Plan.
Step 1. Start the engine. Full throttle may be used during this race.
Step 2. Take off from Meigs Field in Chicago, IL; 17189N 16671E Alt.—592.
Step 3. Climb to an altitude of 1000 feet.
Step 4. Fly six laps around the J. Hancock Building and the Sears Tower. Maintain an airspeed faster than 206.8 knots.
Step 5. Land at Meigs Field.

Flight Debriefing. You will have successfully completed this flight if you:

☐ Flew faster than 206.8 knots.
☐ Safely completed the flight.

38. BENDIX TROPHY RACE 1935

With the 1935 National Air Races coming to an end on 2 September in Cleveland, the start of the Bendix Trophy Race was scheduled for 0001 hours in Burbank, CA. There were nine aircraft at the starting line: Ben Howard in a DGA-6, Jackie Cochran with a Northrop Gamma, Cecil Allen flying a Gee Bee No. 7, Roscoe Turner in a Wedell-Williams Special, Russell Thaw in another Gamma, Earl Ortman piloting a Keith Rider R-3, Royal Leonard with a Gee Bee QED, Roy Hunt in a Lockheed Orion, and Amelia Earhart flying her Lockheed Vega. Only seven of the aircraft started at 0001 hours. Both Allen and Cochran waited until 0300 hours. Unfortunately, as Allen's aircraft left the field it crashed and he was killed. Cochran took off safely, but was thwarted by bad weather in Arizona. Howard won the race with an average speed of 207.4 knots. Turner finished second, just 23 seconds behind the winner.

Flight Setup.

Auto-coordination—Off.
Reality mode—On.
Time: Hours—0. Minutes—01.
Season—Summer.
Cloud layer 2 tops—15,000.
Cloud layer 2 bottoms—10,000.
Cloud layer 1 tops—8500.
Cloud layer 1 bottoms—6325.
Surface wind: Knots—621. Degrees—211.
Reliability factor—95.

Only the Airspeed Indicator, Altimeter, Compass, and Artificial Horizon may be used on the DGA-6.

Flight Objectives. Win the Bendix Trophy Race of 1935.

Filing the Flight Plan.

Step 1. Start the engine. Full throttle may be used during this race.

Step 2. Take off from Burbank, California; 15478N 5861E Alt.—774.

Step 3. Climb to an altitude of 10,000 feet. (Use the slewing controls for this scenario.)

Step 4. Fly to Cleveland. Maintain an airspeed faster than 207.4 knots. (Use 17417N 7446E Alt.—416 for Cleveland.)

Step 5. Land at Cleveland.

Flight Debriefing. You will have successfully completed this flight if you:

☐ Flew faster than 207.4 knots.
☐ Safely completed the flight.

39. HOWARD HUGHES

One barrier that many racing pilots thought to be unbreakable was flying faster than 300 knots. Granted, France's Raymond Delmotte had approached this barrier with a speed of 272.958 knots in a Caudron C460, but even this extreme was still comfortably shy of 300 knots. A young aviator named Howard Hughes teamed fellow designer Richard Palmer and aircraft fabricator Glenn Odekirk with himself to construct an airplane that would be capable of breaking the 300 knot airspeed barrier. Their final result was the Hughes H-1. This sleek aircraft possessed many design innovations that would find their way into some of America's most impressive fighter aircraft of World War II.

On 13 September 1935, Howard Hughes flew the H-1 to a new landplane speed record of 306.018 knots at Santa Ana, California. Hughes would later fly the same aircraft on a record-breaking transcontinental flight from LA-to-New York on 19 January 1937. The entire flight lasted less than 7 1/2 hours.

Flight Setup.
Auto-coordination—Off.
Reality mode—On.
Time: Hours—9. Minutes—00.
Season—Summer.
Surface wind: Knots—8. Degrees—170.
Reliability factor—99.

Only the Airspeed Indicator, Altimeter, Compass, and Artificial Horizon may be used on the Hughes H-1.

The landing gear may be retracted during this scenario.

Flight Objectives. Break the 1935 Speed Record.

Filing the Flight Plan.

Step 1. Start the engine. Full throttle may be used during this race.

Step 2. Take off from Santa Ana, California; 15209N 5965E Alt.—52.

Step 3. Climb to an altitude of 328 feet.

Step 4. Fly in a straight and level attitude at an airspeed faster than 306.018 knots. This high an airspeed can't be properly registered with Flight Simulator's instrument panel. Therefore, hold the airspeed above the 200 knot limit.

Step 5. Return to Santa Ana and repeat this flight six times.

Step 6. Land at Santa Ana.

Flight Debriefing. You will have successfully completed this flight if you:

☐ Flew faster than 306.018 knots.

☐ Safely completed the flight.

40. BENDIX TROPHY RACE 1936

Female pilots were finally exercising their true potential by 1936. Of the seven pilots who participated in the 1936 Bendix Trophy Race, three were women. In fact, Louise Thaden, flying a Staggerwing Beech C-17R, won the race with an average speed of 143.7 knots. Others in the field included Lee Miles in a Gee Bee QED, Ben Howard flying the DGA-6, Joe Jacobson with a Northrop Gamma, Laura Ingalls in a Lockheed Orion, Bill Gulick piloting a Vultee V1A, and Amelia Earhart with a new Lockheed Electra. Roscoe Turner was scheduled to be in the race, but he crashed his Wedell-Williams Special enroute to Cleveland. Ingalls placed second with an average speed of 136.87 knots. This was the first major race where female pilots had placed first and second. A complete female sweep was endangered when Earhart's Electra developed engine problems. In spite of this setback, Amelia still finished fifth.

Flight Setup.

Auto-coordination—Off.

Reality mode—On.

Time: Hours—1. Minutes—00.

Season—Summer.

Cloud layer 1 tops—12,000.

Cloud layer 1 bottoms—6,000.

Surface wind: Knots—221. Degrees—33.

Reliability factor—80.

Only the Airspeed Indicator, Altimeter, Compass, and Artificial Horizon may be used on the Staggerwing Beech C-17R.The landing gear may be retracted during this scenario.

Flight Objectives. Win the Bendix Trophy Race of 1936.

Filing the Flight Plan.

Step 1. Start the engine. Full throttle may be used during this race.

Step 2. Take off from Cleveland (for Cleveland, use 17417N 7446E Alt.-416).

Step 3. Climb to an altitude of 10,000 feet. (Use the slewing controls in this scenario.)

Step 4. Fly to Burbank, California; 15478N 5861E Alt.—774. Maintain an average airspeed of 143.7 knots.

Step 5. Land at Burbank.

Flight Debriefing. You will have successfully completed this flight if you:

☐ Flew the complete course with a speed faster than 143.7 knots.
☐ Safely completed the flight. Ben Howard and Joe Jacobson were not so lucky. Both pilots had their aircraft crash during the race.

Chapter 10

World War II—Europe

41. STUKA STRIKE

Just 21 years after the signing of the Armistice, the world was plunged back into war at 0415 hours on 1 September 1939. Germany sent seven armies into Poland on an enormous pincer action designed to surround the surprised Polish Army. A vast, well-trained Luftwaffe supported the advances of the German Army. Communication centers, airfields, and supply lines were attacked by the German bombers, while the ground troops continued to close their ring around the Polish Army.

These invasion tactics marked a distinct turn from the trench warfare of World War I. Along with these new tactics, special aircraft had been designed, which were capable of supporting a mobile army. The Junkers Ju 87B-2 *Sturzkampfflugzeug* (or Stuka) dive bomber was an excellent example of Germany's new offensive Luftwaffe. Offering only token opposition, Poland was defeated in less than four weeks.

Flight Setup.

Europe 1917—On.

Only the Airspeed Indicator, Altimeter, Compass, and Artificial Horizon may be used on the Ju 87B-2.

The landing gear may not be retracted during this scenario.

Flight Objectives. Bomb a Polish airfield.

Filing the Flight Plan.

Step 1. Start the engine. Full throttle may be used during this mission. Declare war by pressing the W key (or the Shift + W combination).

Step 2. Take off from the Luftwaffe base. Jettison three of the bombs by pressing the X key (or the Shift + X combination). Only two bombs will be needed for this mission.

Step 3. Climb to an altitude of 7,000 feet.

Step 4. Locate the primary Polish airfield.

Step 5. Making a diving attack on the airfield, drop your bombs (Fig. 10-1).

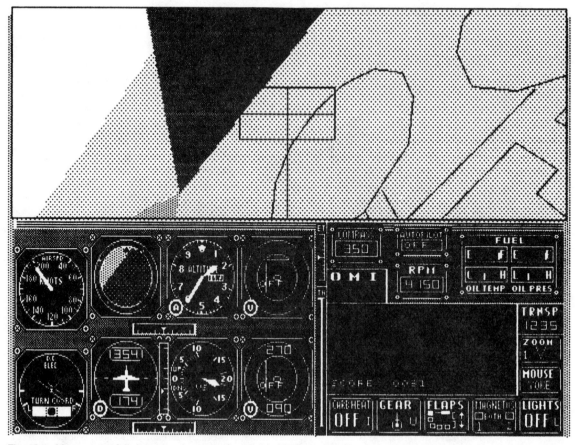

Fig. 10-1. After successfully bombing the enemy's airfield, this Stuka is pulling out of its dive to engage the Polish fighters.

Step 6. Avoid the enemy fighters and return to your base.
Flight Debriefing. You will have successfully completed this flight if you:

☐ Successfully hit the enemy airfield. This result will have to be confirmed visually. Flight Simulator does not record bomb hits on the airfields.
☐ Safely completed the flight.

42. BLITZKRIEG

Having conquered Poland, Germany turned its sights on France. Assuming that Germany would launch its invasion across the Germany/France border, the French Army was fortified in a defensive posture along the Maginot Line. Instead of forcing a direct confrontation, 75 German divisions swept through the Netherlands and Belgium in a race for the coast. This move caught both England and France off guard. The bulk of the Allied armies in northern France retreated to the port city of Dunkirk. A massive rescue effort saved 336,000 British and French soldiers from capture. Having secured the northern coast of France, the German Army turned south towards Paris. Under an air superiority cover of Messerschmitt Bf 109E-3s, the German Army forced Paris to surrender on 14 June 1940. France had been defeated in less than six weeks.

Flight Setup.

Europe 1917—On.

Only the Airspeed Indicator, Altimeter, Compass, and Artificial Horizon may be used on the Bf 109E-3.

The landing gear may be retracted during this scenario.

Flight Objectives. Engage French fighters near Paris.

Filing the Flight Plan.

Step 1. Start the engine. Full throttle may be used during this mission. Declare war by pressing the W key (or the Shift + W combination).

Step 2. Take off from the Luftwaffe base.

Step 3. Climb to an altitude of 9,500 feet.

Step 4. Fly an air superiority mission over France.

Step 5. Engage any fighters that attack you.

Step 6. Return to your base.

Flight Debriefing. You will have successfully completed this flight if you:

☐ Engaged enemy fighters near Paris.

☐ Safely completed the flight.

43. BOMBEN BRITAIN

With Europe caught in the final throes of its blitzkrieg death grip, England remained the sole obstacle to preventing Nazi world domination. Preceded by a series of preliminary aerial attacks, the Luftwaffe began its first major concerted bombing of Britain on 8 August 1940. The Battle of Britain had begun.

The principal aircraft used by the Luftwaffe during these missions were large formations of Ju 87B-2 bombers escorted by Messerschmitt Bf 110C-1 Zerstörer fighters. The losses suffered at the hands of the RAF from this bomber/fighter arrangement were staggering. For example, in August, when the Luftwaffe mounted its *Adlerangriff* (''Attack of the Eagles'') campaign, 120 Bf 110Cs were destroyed by British Spitfires and Hurricanes. Even when the Bf 110C was moved into a fighter/bomber role, the results were less than satisfactory.

Flight Setup.

Europe 1917—On.

Only the Airspeed Indicator, Altimeter, Compass, and Artificial Horizon may be used on the Bf 110C-1.

The landing gear may be retracted during this scenario.

Flight Objectives. Engage British fighters near London.

Filing the Flight Plan.

Step 1. Start the engine. Full throttle may be used during this mission. Declare war by pressing the W key (or the Shift + W combination).

Step 2. Take off from the Luftwaffe base.

Step 3. Climb to an altitude of 3500 feet.

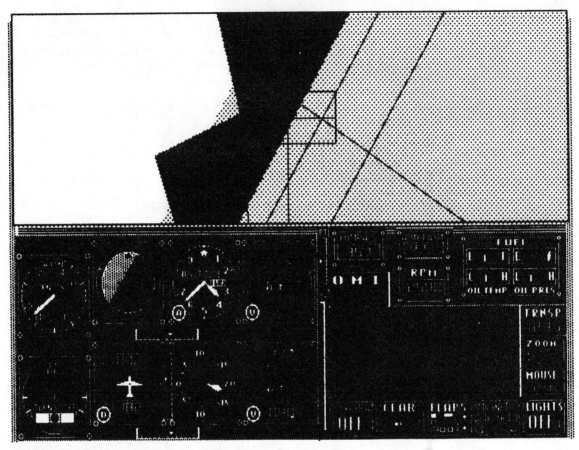

Fig. 10-2. This Bf 110C-1 has a British Hurricane in its gunsight.

Step 4. Fly a "free hunt" mission over England.
Step 5. Engage any fighters that attack you (Fig. 10-2).
Step 6. Return to your base.
Flight Debriefing. You will have successfully completed this flight if you:

☐ Engaged enemy fighters over England.
☐ Safely completed the flight.

44. TALLYHO

Germany's initial air assault posed numerous problems for the RAF. The Luftwaffe's primary goal was to destroy the British air defenses and industry through a concentrated aerial bombardment with 2,800 aircraft. Britain's head of Fighter Command, Air Chief Marshal Dowding, met this threat with 640 frontline fighters. Additionally, early warning radar stations were placed along the coast for detecting the waves of approaching German bombers.

Initially the Battle of Britain went in the Luftwaffe's favor, with 77 of Britain's fighters lost in July 1940. Clever squadron rotation by Dowding, however, saved many of the RAF's pilots from flying severely damaged aircraft. This replenishment program, coupled with the Luftwaffe's switch to civilian targets, gave Britain's Supermarine Spitfire Mk IA pilots the edge they needed in quashing the German High Command's hopes for German air superiority over England.

Flight Setup.

Europe 1917—On.

Only the Airspeed Indicator, Altimeter, Compass, and Artificial Horizon may be used on the Spitfire.

The landing gear may be retracted during this scenario.

Flight Objectives. Engage German fighters near Newcastle.

Filing the Flight Plan.

Step 1. Start the engine. Full throttle may be used during this mission. Declare war by pressing the W key (or the Shift + W combination).

Step 2. Take off from Biggen Hill.

Step 3. Climb to an altitude of 9000 feet.

Step 4. Fly a defensive mission over England.

Step 5. Engage any fighters that attack you.

Step 6. Return to your base.

Flight Debriefing. You will have successfully completed this flight if you:

☐ Engaged the Luftwaffe over England.
☐ Safely completed the flight.

45. TORCH

Halting the German advance at the coast of England did not prevent the Nazis from extending their domain. Large portions of North Africa, eastern Europe, and Russia were being overrun by the Axis armies in 1941 and 1942. It was in the deserts of North Africa, however, that the English were finally able to take the offensive against the Nazis. General Bernard Montgomery, commanding 8th Army, had forced Rommel's Afrika Korps into an uncharacteristic retreat at El Alamein. A total German rout was ensured when American and British forces landed at two points in Morocco and Algeria during Operation Torch. Vital Algerian airfields supported the combined RAF and USAAF (US Army Air Force), as Curtiss P-40E Warhawks and Hawker Hurricane Mk IIDs pounded the retreating German and Italian Armies.

Flight Setup.

Europe 1917—On.

Only the Airspeed Indicator, Altimeter, Compass, and Artificial Horizon may be used on the P-40E.

The landing gear may be retracted during this scenario.

Flight Objectives. Bomb an Afrika Korps fuel depot.

Filing the Flight Plan.

Step 1. Start the engine. Full throttle may be used during this mission. Declare war by pressing the W key (or the Shift + W combination).

Step 2. Take off from Algeria. Jettison three of your bombs by pressing the X key (or the

Shift + X combination).
Step 3. Climb to an altitude of 2000 feet.
Step 4. Fly to the primary fuel depot.
Step 5. Drop your two bombs on the depot.
Step 6. Return to your base.
Flight Debriefing. You will have successfully completed this flight if you:

☐ Destroyed the Afrika Korps fuel depot.
☐ Safely completed the flight.

46. BAYTOWN

After losing its hold in North Africa, the German Army began a slow but steady retreat back to Europe. The final resting place for the bulk of the defeated German and Italian forces was in Italy. Determined to make yet another final stand, enormous fortifications were installed throughout the Italian peninsula. Electing to invade Italy in gradual steps, the Allies liberated Sicily in early August 1943. From this steppingstone, the combined American and British invasion force attempted to cross the Strait of Messina.

Operation Baytown began on 3 September with the British 8th Army landing on the European continent in Italy. Continuous bombing by USAAF North American B-25C medium bombers cut the enemies' supply lines and allowed for a rapid advance by the British Army.

Flight Setup.

Europe 1917—On.

Only the Airspeed Indicator, Altimeter, Compass, and Artificial Horizon may be used on the B-25C.

The landing gear may be retracted during this scenario.

Flight Objectives. Cut the German supply lines.

Fig. 10-3. Following takeoff, this B-25C-20 tries to gain altitude.

Filing the Flight Plan.

Step 1. Start the engine. Full throttle may be used during this mission. Declare war by pressing the W key (or the Shift + W combination).

Step 2. Take off from Sicily. Jettison one of your bombs by pressing the X key (or the Shift + X combination).

Step 3. Climb to an altitude of 5000 feet (Fig. 10-3).

Step 4. Fly to the primary fuel depot.

Step 5. Drop all of your bombs on the depot from a level attitude.

Step 6. Return to your base.

Flight Debriefing. You will have successfully completed this flight if you:

☐ Cut the Axis supply line.
☐ Safely completed the flight.

47. PLOESTI

Eliminating the Axis synthetic fuel development programs was one of several methods used for dismantling the German war machine. Large formations of American Boeing B-17G heavy bombers were the usual method for dealing with these strategic targets. In certain cases, well-protected targets were able to endure large-scale USAAF bombing attacks with relatively little damage. The fuel refineries at Ploesti, Rumania, were literally flattened from numerous raids by 15th Air Force bombers. These raids proved ineffective in halting the production of fuel, however.

Therefore, a special group of Lockheed P-38J Lightnings (Fig. 10-4) under the command of Lt. Colonel William P. Litton took off on 10 June 1944 for a low-level bombing mission at Ploesti. Battling enemy fighters, flak, and smoke, the P-38Js scored several direct hits on the Rumanian oil cracking facility.

Flight Setup.

Europe 1917—On.

Only the Airspeed Indicator, Altimeter, Compass, and Artificial Horizon may be used on the P-38J.

The landing gear may be retracted during this scenario.

Flight Objectives. Bomb Ploesti.

Filing the Flight Plan.

Step 1. Start the engine. Full throttle may be used during this mission. Declare war by pressing the W key (or the Shift + W combination).

Step 2. Take off from Italy. Jettison three of your bombs by pressing the X key (or the Shift + X combination).

Step 3. Climb to an altitude of 500 feet.

Step 4. Fly to the secondary fuel depot. Climb to 1500 feet.

Step 5. Drop both of your bombs on the depot from a shallow dive.

Step 6. Return to your base.

Flight Debriefing. You will have successfully completed this flight if you:

☐ Destroyed Ploesti.
☐ Safely completed the flight.

Fig. 10-4. A young Lt. A. D. Prochnow (the author's father) standing next to a 15th Air Force P-38J.

48. SHUTTLE TO RUSSIA

As the German Army was forced back to the borders of Germany, strategic targets were located farther from Allied bases in England and Italy. The long distances that were traveled by the bombers and their fighter escort seriously tested the endurance of the flight crews. In an effort to increase the bombing range of the B-17Gs and their North American P-51D Mustang (Fig. 10-5) escorts, one-way missions were flown over Germany with the bomber force landing at support bases in Russia. This "shuttle run" would then be repeated after the aircraft had been refueled.

The first shuttle mission by the 15th Air Force occurred on 2 June 1944, with four bomb groups and one fighter group attacking the railway yards at Debrecen, Hungary. After a brief stay at Kiev, Russia, this same formation returned to Italy on 11 June 1944.

Flight Setup.

Europe 1917—On.

Only the Airspeed Indicator, Altimeter, Compass, and Artificial Horizon may be used on the P-51D.

The landing gear may be retracted during this scenario.

Flight Objectives. Fly fighter escort on a shuttle mission.

Filing the Flight Plan.

Step 1. Start the engine. Full throttle may be used during this mission. Declare war by pressing the W key (or the Shift + W combination).

Step 2. Take off from Italy. Jettison all of your bombs by pressing the X key (or the Shift + X combination).

Step 3. Climb to an altitude of 9000 feet.

Step 4. Fly to the primary factory.

Step 5. Engage any enemy fighters that appear.

Step 6. Return to the secondary Allied base.

Step 7. After you have been refueled, repeat the above steps, but land at the main base when you have completed the mission.

Flight Debriefing. You will have successfully completed this flight if you:

☐ Escorted shuttle bombers to and from Russia.
☐ Safely completed the flight.

Fig. 10-5. Shuttling P-51Ds into Russia strengthened Allied air superiority over Germany.

49. FIGHTER SWEEP

By late 1944 and early 1945, the American and British ground forces were sprinting through France and into Germany. Advanced fighter bases in France and Belgium provided USAAF and RAF aircraft with complete air superiority in the skies of western Europe. This aerial freedom of operation gave American fighter/bomber squadrons unlimited opportunities for launching continuous attacks against the shrinking German supply lines. Republic P-47D-25 Thunderbolts carried out the lion's share of these ground interdiction duties.

Flight Setup.

Europe 1917—On.

Only the Airspeed Indicator, Altimeter, Compass, and Artificial Horizon may be used on the P-47D.

The landing gear may be retracted during this scenario.

Flight Objectives. Attack German ground targets.

Filing the Flight Plan.

Step 1. Start the engine. Full throttle may be used during this mission. Declare war by pressing the W key (or the Shift + W combination).

Step 2. Take off from Italy. Jettison two of your bombs by pressing the X key (or the Shift + X combination).

Step 3. Climb to an altitude of 1500 feet.

Step 4. Fly to the primary factory.

Step 5. Drop all three of your bombs on the factory from a shallow dive.

Step 6. Return to your base.

Flight Debriefing. You will have successfully completed this flight if you:

☐ Destroyed the factory.

☐ Safely completed the flight.

50. FOGGIA PLAIN

The unsung heros of the long-range strategic bombing of Germany were the members of the

Fig. 10-6. Life on the Foggia Plain was far from comfortable.

15th Air Force. Operating from primitive bases on Italy's Foggia Plain, B-17Gs and Consolidated B-24Hs flew many of the toughest missions in World War II (Fig. 10-6). Attacking heavily defended targets such as Ploesti, Regensburg, Wiener-Neustadt, and Berlin, the 15th Air Force suffered some outstanding losses. The cost imposed on the crews of the 15th Air Force is typified by the loss of 318 aircraft in July 1944 while bombing Ploesti. This number is significantly higher than the losses experienced by the England-based 8th Air Force.

Other than strategic bombing missions, the 15th Air Force was also instrumental in espionage and insurgency tactics by supplying the various resistance movements throughout Hungary, Rumania, and Italy with arms and assistance. In the final days of the war in Europe, the 15th Air Force was used for dropping supplies to various prisoner of war camps in southern Germany. Later, these same aircraft, which had been bombing Germany just one month prior, would be used for airlifting American prisoners home.

Flight Setup.

Europe 1917—On.

Only the Airspeed Indicator, Altimeter, Compass, and Artificial Horizon may be used on the B-17G (Fig. 10-7).

The landing gear may be retracted during this scenario.

Flight Objectives. Bomb Berlin.

Filing the Flight Plan.

Step 1. Start the engine. Full throttle may be used during this mission. Declare war by pressing the W key (or the Shift + W combination).

Fig. 10-7. The cockpit of the B-17G.

Step 2. Take off from the Foggia Plain.

Step 3. Climb to an altitude of 10,000 feet.

Step 4. Fly to the primary factory.

Step 5. Drop all of your bombs on the factory from a level attitude.

Step 6. Return to your base.

Flight Debriefing. You will have successfully completed this flight if you:

☐ Destroyed the Berlin factory.

☐ Safely completed the flight.

Chapter 11

World War II—Pacific

51. FLYING TIGERS

Even before the Japanese attacked Pearl Harbor, a group of 230 Americans under the command of Major Claire Lee Chennault were preparing to go to war with this foe. Flying from bases in Kunming and Mingaladon, China, this group, known as the Flying Tigers or American Volunteer Group (AVG), claimed 286 Japanese aircraft destroyed with their Curtiss P-40Bs. As President Roosevelt became aware of the value of this group, new P-40E aircraft were sent to the beleaguered Flying Tiger pilots. Along with these new aircraft came a new name for the unit, China Air Task Force, and a promotion for Chennault to the rank of Major General.

Flight Setup.

Europe 1917—On.

Only the Airspeed Indicator, Altimeter, Compass, and Artificial Horizon may be used on the P-40E.

The landing gear may be retracted during this scenario.

Flight Objectives. Destroy Japanese fighters over Burma.

Filing the Flight Plan.

Step 1. Start the engine. Full throttle may be used during this mission. Declare war by pressing the W key (or the Shift + W combination).

Step 2. Take off from Kunming.

Step 3. Climb to an altitude of 1500 feet.

Step 4. Fly to the secondary enemy airfield.

Step 5. Engage the enemy fighters.

Step 6. Return to your base.

Flight Debriefing. You will have successfully completed this flight if you:

☐ Intercepted the enemy fighters.
☐ Safely completed the flight.

52. ISLAND HOPPING

American industry was quick to rebound from the staggering blow that was delivered by the Japanese aerial attack on Pearl Harbor. Determined to recapture several of the key island groups in the central Pacific, Rear Admiral Charles A. Pownall lead his Task Force 50 in Operation Galvanic against the Gilbert islands. Supported by several fleet aircraft carriers and light carriers, Pownall divided his force into four separate assault groups. Beginning on 19 November 1943, the major invasion of the Gilberts began. Grumman F6F-5 Hellcat fighters intercepted any Japanese aircraft that attempted to attack the invasion force. This aerial umbrella shot down 58 enemy aircraft over a two-day period.

Flight Setup.

Europe 1917—On.

Only the Airspeed Indicator, Altimeter, Compass, and Artificial Horizon may be used on the F6F-5.

The landing gear may be retracted during this scenario.

Flight Objectives. Intercept all enemy fighters.

Filing the Flight Plan.

Step 1. Start the engine. Full throttle may be used during this mission. Declare war by pressing the W key (or the Shift + W combination).

Step 2. Take off from the *USS Essex.* (Use your imagination for converting the land airbase into a rolling carrier's deck.)

Step 3. Climb to an altitude of 3500 feet.

Step 4. Fly to the secondary enemy airfield.

Step 5. Engage the enemy fighters.

Step 6. Return to your carrier.

Flight Debriefing. You will have successfully completed this flight if you:

☐ Prevented enemy fighters from disrupting the invasion.
☐ Safely completed the flight.

53. BLACK SHEEP

Once an island or an island chain had been recaptured, USN Seabees (Construction Battalion) built land-based airfields. These fields enabled transport and cargo aircraft to deliver supplies more efficiently to the ocean-based carrier task forces. Another use for these forward airbases was to launch fighter and fighter/bomber aircraft against other Japanese-held islands.

Frequently, these advanced bases were used by U.S. Marine fighter squadrons. The exploits of a Marine air squadron commanded by the colorful Major Gregory "Pappy" Boyington, who shot down 28 enemy aircraft, fueled the media's desire to follow the aerial adventures over the PTO (Pacific Theater of Operations). Flying the beautiful Chance Vought F4U-1D Corsair (Fig. 11-1), VMF-214, also known as the Black Sheep, racked up several impressive victories from their Guadalcanal base.

Flight Setup.

Europe 1917—On.

Only the Airspeed Indicator, Altimeter, Compass, and Artificial Horizon may be used on the F4U-1D.

Fig. 11-1. A Chance Vought F4U Corsair with its wings still folded prepares for takeoff with three P-51Ds.

The landing gear may be retracted during this scenario.

Flight Objectives. Destroy three fighters over Rabaul.

Filing the Flight Plan.

Step 1. Start the engine. Full throttle may be used during this mission. Declare war by pressing the W key (or the Shift + W combination).

Step 2. Take off from Guadalcanal.

Step 3. Climb to an altitude of 5000 feet.

Step 4. Fly to the secondary enemy airfield.

Step 5. Shoot down three enemy fighters.

Step 6. Return to your base.

Flight Debriefing. You will have successfully completed this flight if you:

☐ Destroyed three enemy fighters.
☐ Safely completed the flight.

54. DIVINE WIND

As the American domination of the air slowly enveloped the Pacific, the Japanese Army and Naval air forces resorted to a new tactic. Delving into an ancient tale that dealt with the salvation of feudal Japan from a similar invasion force, Japan called on its pilots to volunteer for special suicide missions. Known as *kamikazes* (roughly translated as "divine wind"), these pilots would fly their aircraft directly into the American targets. These targets were usually major capital ships such as fleet aircraft carriers, cruisers, and battleships.

For the most part, the kamikazes used older aircraft models that had been loaded with enormous explosive payloads. As the war wore on, however, even some of the finer frontline fighters, such as the Kawasaki Ki-61, were pressed into kamikaze service.

Flight Setup.

Europe 1917—On.

Only the Airspeed Indicator, Altimeter, Compass, and Artificial Horizon may be used on the Ki-61.

The landing gear may be retracted during this scenario.

Flight Objectives. Make a kamikaze attack on an American fuel depot.

Filing the Flight Plan.

Step 1. Start the engine. Full throttle may be used during this mission. Declare war by pressing the W key (or the Shift + W combination).

Step 2. Take off from Okinawa.

Step 3. Climb to an altitude of 2000 feet.

Step 4. Fly to the secondary enemy fuel depot.

Step 5. Dive on the target and release one bomb prior to hitting the depot. (Press the X key or the Shift + X combination.)

Step 6. *Don't* return to your base.

Flight Debriefing. You will have successfully completed this flight if you:

☐ Destroyed the fuel depot.
☐ Did *not* safely complete the flight.

55. FORAGER

American naval forces continued to recapture islands along a direct route to Japan. Following several decisive U.S. naval victories, Operation Forager was prepared as an assault of Saipan and Guam. On 11 June 1944, 208 F6F-5s were launched for strikes against the Japanese air forces. A total of 38 Japanese aircraft was destroyed. Four days later, U.S. Marines invaded Saipan. A rapidly launched Japanese counterattacking naval task force was sailed in the direction of Saipan.

Reacting to this approaching threat, Admiral Spruance broke up his Saipan/Guam invasion force and awaited the Japanese fleet. Continuing their attack on Saipan while the naval forces battled each other in the open ocean, the U.S. Marines completely recaptured Saipan on 9 July 1944 with 14,000 American casualties and 30,000 Japanese killed.

Flight Setup.

Europe 1917—On.

Only the Airspeed Indicator, Altimeter, Compass, and Artificial Horizon may be used on the F6F-5.

The landing gear may be retracted during this scenario.

Flight Objectives. Attack enemy fighters over Saipan.

Filing the Flight Plan.

Step 1. Start the engine. Full throttle may be used during this mission. Declare war by pressing the W key (or the Shift + W combination).

Step 2. Take off from the *USS Princeton*. (Once again, imagine that you're on the deck of an aircraft carrier.)

Step 3. Climb to an altitude of 7500 feet.

Step 4. Fly to the secondary enemy airfield.

Step 5. Engage the enemy fighters.

Step 6. Return to your carrier.

Flight Debriefing. You will have successfully completed this flight if you:

☐ Engaged the enemy fighters.

☐ Safely completed the flight.

56. IWO JIMA

The last major island in the chain to Japan was a five-mile-long bit of volcanic rock called Iwo Jima. Rear Admiral Durgin commanded Task Force 52.2, which was figured for the actual invasion of Iwo Jima. Providing air support for Durgin's force was Vice Admiral Mitscher's Task Force 58. On 19 February 1945 the invasion of Iwo Jima began. In one day, 40,000 Marines were placed ashore.

Less than 14 days were needed for eliminating the Japanese resistance, but the price was heavy. Two major fleet aircraft carriers were seriously damaged by kamikaze attacks. While the *USS Saratoga* was salvageable, the *USS Bismarck Sea* was lost with 34 aircraft and 218 crewmen. The Marines involved with the ground fighting, on the other hand, experienced 5,000 casualties.

Flight Setup.

Europe 1917—On.

Only the Airspeed Indicator, Altimeter, Compass, and Artificial Horizon may be used on the F6F-5.

The landing gear may be retracted during this scenario.

Flight Objectives. Shoot down four enemy fighters.

Filing the Flight Plan.

Step 1. Start the engine. Full throttle may be used during this mission. Declare war by pressing the W key (or the Shift + W combination).

Step 2. Take off from the *USS Enterprise*. (Yes, you're still on the deck of an aircraft carrier.)

Step 3. Climb to an altitude of 6000 feet.

Step 4. Fly to the secondary enemy airfield.

Step 5. Engage the enemy fighters. Shoot down four planes.

Step 6. Return to your carrier.

Flight Debriefing. You will have successfully completed this flight if you:

☐ Shot down four enemy fighters.

☐ Safely completed the flight.

57. BONG

In a theater that was dominated by ocean, it is indeed ironic that the leading American ace would appear in the PTO as a land-based P-38J pilot. Assigned to the 5th Air Force, 49th Fighter Group, Major Richard Ira Bong scored 40 kills on over 146 missions. After his 40th kill, General Arnold ordered Bong to return to the United States. Tragically, Bong was later killed during the testing of the USAAF's new jet fighter, the Lockheed P-80 Shooting Star.

Flight Setup.

Europe 1917—On.

Only the Airspeed Indicator, Altimeter, Compass, and Artificial Horizon may be used on the P-38J.

The landing gear may be retracted during this scenario.

Flight Objectives. Destroy five fighters.

Filing the Flight Plan.

Step 1. Start the engine. Full throttle may be used during this mission. Declare war by pressing the W key (or the Shift + W combination).

Step 2. Take off from Leyte.

Step 3. Climb to an altitude of 9000 feet.

Step 4. Fly to the secondary enemy airfield.

Step 5. Shoot down five enemy fighters.

Step 6. Return to your base.

Flight Debriefing. You will have successfully completed this flight if you:

☐ Destroyed five enemy fighters.
☐ Safely completed the flight.

58. TEN-GO

Following its regular routine for the invasion of an island, American forces began their attack of Okinawa on 1 April 1945. Unknown to the Task Force, Japan had organized a special suicide counterattack coded Operation Ten-Go. Ten-Go was a joint air and sea kamikaze venture comprising 4500 aircraft, the battleship *Yamato*, and numerous support vessels. Most of the kamikaze aircraft were destroyed before they ever reached their intended targets. Likewise, the *Yamato* was intercepted in open sea by fighters, dive bombers, and torpedo bombers from Task Force 58. Ten direct torpedo hits and five direct bombs hits were needed to sink the last of Japan's great ships. Virtually the entire crew died with the *Yamato*, a total of 2498 men.

Flight Setup.

Europe 1917—On.

Only the Airspeed Indicator, Altimeter, Compass, and Artificial Horizon may be used on the Mitsubishi A6M Reisen.

The landing gear may be retracted during this scenario.

Flight Objectives. Make a kamikaze attack on Okinawa.

Filing the Flight Plan.

Step 1. Start the engine. Full throttle may be used during this mission. Declare war by pressing the W key (or the Shift + W combination).

Step 2. Take off from Okinawa.

Step 3. Climb to an altitude of 2000 feet.

Step 4. Fly to the secondary enemy factory.

Step 5. Dive on the target and release one bomb prior to hitting the target. (Press the X key or the Shift + X combination.)

Step 6. *Don't* return to your base.

Flight Debriefing. You will have successfully completed this flight if you:

☐ Destroyed the factory.
☐ Did not safely complete the flight.

59. ZIPPER

In direct contrast to the war in Europe, the United States was virtually single-handedly responsible for the victory over Japan in the PTO. The only other Ally that was making a strong effort at fighting the Japanese was Great Britain and the members of her Commonwealth (e.g., Australia and New Zealand). This contribution found England fighting mainly in Burma and China.

After suffering some devastating early defeats, the British came back with a vengeance in July 1944. Air Chief Marshal Sir Richard Peirse directed a powerful 90 squadron attack that destroyed both the Japanese air forces and, to a large extent, their ground forces as well. By 31 July 1945, the Japanese Army and combined air forces had been defeated in Burma. The invasions of Malaya and Singapore were being planned as Operation Zipper when the Japanese surrendered and the war ended.

Flight Setup.

Europe 1917—On.

Only the Airspeed Indicator, Altimeter, Compass, and Artificial Horizon may be used on the Hawker MK IIC Hurricane.

The landing gear may be retracted during this scenario.

Flight Objectives. Shoot down ten enemy fighters.

Filing the Flight Plan.

Step 1. Start the engine. Full throttle may be used during this mission. Declare war by pressing the W key (or the Shift + W combination).

Step 2. Take off from Morotai.

Step 3. Climb to an altitude of 7000 feet.

Step 4. Fly to the secondary enemy airfield.

Step 5. Fly as many sorties or missions as is necessary for you to destroy ten enemy fighters.

Step 6. Return to your base and refuel and rearm after each sortie.

Flight Debriefing. You will have successfully completed this flight if you:

☐ Destroyed ten enemy fighters.
☐ Safely completed the flight.

60. SUPERFORTRESS

By 20 January 1945, only Japan itself remained to be invaded. After studying the feasibility of such an invasion, the U.S. opted for a less costly destruction of the Japanese war effort. Long-range strategic bombing attacks by high-altitude Boeing B-29 Superfortresses were used to eliminate every possible war production target from Japan.

Along with these daylight bombing raids, Major General Curtis E. LeMay designed a plan for low-level (10,000 feet) night incendiary attacks. By reducing the defensive armament of the B-29s, larger payloads of the incendiary bombs could be lifted over the target. These "fire raids," which began on 9 March 1945, completely engulfed the cities of Tokyo, Yawata, Osaka, and Yokohama. In all, over 500,000 Japanese were killed in these night attacks. Finally, two single B-29s dropped one atomic bomb each on Hiroshima and Nagasaki on 6 August 1945 and 9 August 1945, respectively. World War II had ended.

Flight Setup.

Europe 1917—On.

Only the Airspeed Indicator, Altimeter, Compass, and Artificial Horizon may be used on the B-29.

The landing gear may be retracted during this scenario.

Flight Objectives. Bomb three targets over Japan.

Filing the Flight Plan.

Step 1. Start the engine. Full throttle may be used during this mission. Declare war by pressing the W key (or the Shift + W combination).

Step 2. Take off from Tinian.

Step 3. Climb to an altitude of 10,000 feet.

Step 4. Fly to the secondary enemy targets (two factories and one fuel depot).

Step 5. Fly three sorties or missions to destroy the three targets. Press the X key (or the Shift + X combination) for dropping your payload.

Step 6. Return to Tinian and refuel and rearm after each sortie.

Flight Debriefing. You will have successfully completed this flight if you:

☐ Destroyed the three enemy targets.
☐ Safely completed the flight.

Chapter 12

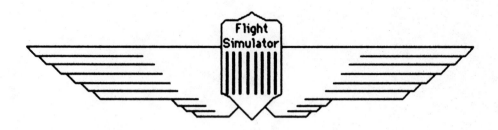

Civil Aviation

61. CESSNA

Clyde Cessna didn't become interested in aviation until he witnessed an aerial demonstration in 1910. Eager to learn the "art" of flight, Cessna purchased a fuselage from Willis McCormick for McCormick's Queen Monoplane. After adding his own wings, empennage, and engine, Cessna was ready for the first test flight. Unfortunately, Cyle lacked any flying experience. Therefore, these beginning flights in the modified Queen Monoplane served as both flight education for the pilot and flight testing for the aircraft.

Following success at barnstorming, Cessna entered into a business arrangement with Lloyd Stearman and Walter Beech and formed the Travel Air Manufacturing Company in Wichita, Kansas. A falling out among the three partners sent Cessna out to design and market his own airplanes. In 1927, the first Cessna, the Model A, was released by the Cessna-Roos Aircraft Company. After market acceptance of the design and one final partnership change, the Cessna Aircraft Company was born.

Flight Setup.
Auto-coordination—Off.
Reality mode—On.
Time: Hours—9. Minutes—00.
Season—Summer.
Surface wind: Knots—17. Degrees—78.
Reliability factor—90.
Only the Airspeed Indicator, Altimeter, Compass, and Artificial Horizon may be used on the Cessna 140.

Flight Objectives. Fly the Cessna 140.
Filing the Flight Plan.
Step 1. Start the engine. Full throttle may be used during this flight.

Step 2. Take off from Wichita, KS; 15460N 13250E Alt.—1332.

Step 3. Climb to an altitude of 8000 feet.

Step 4. Fly to Hutchinson, KS; 15654N 13123E Alt.—1542.

Step 5. Land at Hutchinson.

Flight Debriefing. You will have successfully completed this flight if you:

☐ Flew the Cessna 140 to Hutchinson, KS.

☐ Safely completed the flight.

62. PIPER

William T. Piper, Sr. made his first attempt in the aviation industry as a financial partner in the Taylor Brothers Aircraft Company in 1929. After several failures at building a salable aircraft design, the company went bankrupt in 1931. In spite of its management troubles, Piper felt that the company still had some good aircraft designs and purchased all of the company's assets for $1000. Piper retained both the original company's name and its chief engineer, C. G. Taylor. Their first success was the E-2 Cub, which sold for $1325 in 1932. In 1935, Taylor left the company and started his own aircraft manufacturing plant in Alliance, Ohio.

Piper continued to improve on the popular Cub design and released the J-2 in 1936. The following year, a fire at the factory forced Piper to relocate to Lock Haven, Pennsylvania. The company's name was also changed with this move and became the Piper Aircraft Corporation. Interestingly enough, the basic Cub design continued to sell into the 1980s. The final version, the Super Cub PA-18, sports many technological improvements, but adheres closely to the graceful lines of the original 1932 aircraft.

Flight Setup.

Auto-coordination—Off.

Reality mode—On.

Time: Hours—15. Minutes—30.

Season—Fall.

Surface wind: Knots—22. Degrees—121.

Reliability factor—90.

Only the Airspeed Indicator, Altimeter, Compass, and Artificial Horizon may be used on the Piper Super Cub.

Flight Objectives. Fly the Piper Super Cub.

Filing the Flight Plan.

Step 1. Start the engine. Full throttle may be used during this flight.

Step 2. Take off from John F. Kennedy International Airport; 17034N 21065E Alt.—12.

Step 3. Climb to an altitude of 5500 feet.

Step 4. Fly to Martha's Vineyard, MA; 17490N 22043E Alt.—68.

Step 5. Land at Martha's Vineyard.

Flight Debriefing. You will have successfully completed this flight if you:

☐ Flew the Piper Super Cub to Martha's Vineyard.

☐ Safely completed the flight.

63. STINSON

Eddie Stinson made a definitive start in civilian aviation by building a four-place biplane at his Detroit, Michigan, factory in 1925. Known as a "Detroiter," the biplane made its first successful flight on 25 January 1926. Several important financial investors witnessed the flight and subsequently provided Stinson with enough capital for forming the Stinson Aircraft Corporation. Full production of the Detroiter started in August 1926.

This design was followed by the SM-1, a $12,000 six-place monoplane, which marked the first of Stinson's long line of profitable monoplanes. Always preferring to demonstrate his own aircraft designs, Stinson was killed on 26 January 1932 in a crash of his new Stinson Model R. Following Stinson's death, the company continued to prosper for another 17 years and left a distinctive mark on aviation with the beautiful SR-7 (Fig. 12-1).

Flight Setup.
Auto-coordination—Off.
Reality mode—On.
Time: Hours—13. Minutes—30.
Season—Winter.
Surface wind: Knots—12. Degrees—39.
Reliability factor—90.

Only the Airspeed Indicator, Altimeter, Compass, and Artificial Horizon may be used on the SR-7.

Fig. 12-1. A gull-winged Stinson SR-7. This beautiful aircraft has a red color scheme with cream accents.

Flight Objectives. Fly the Stinson SR-7.

Filing the Flight Plan.

Step 1. Start the engine. Full throttle may be used during this flight.

Step 2. Take off from Meigs Field in Chicago, IL; 17189N 16671E Alt.—592.

Step 3. Climb to an altitude of 1250 feet.

Step 4. Fly to Chicago-Midway Airport; 17156N 16628E Alt.—619.

Step 5. Land at Midway.

Flight Debriefing. You will have successfully completed this flight if you:

☐ Flew the SR-7 to Midway.

☐ Safely completed the flight.

64. FAIRCHILD

Fairchild Airplane Manufacturing Corporation was founded by two brothers, Walter L. Fairchild and Sherman Fairchild. The company was started by Walter, who personally built the first production aircraft in 1911. This initial effort was unique in two aspects. First, the design was a monoplane, in direct contrast with the accepted biplane standard of that era. The second exemplary feature of these early Fairchilds was in their use of steel tubing. Once again, this construction technique was a bold example of a pioneering design that contradicted the accepted aircraft design norms.

In 1925, the Fairchild-Caminez Engine Corporation was structured as a subsidiary of the Fairchild Airplane Manufacturing Corporation. The engine produced by the company, the Fairchild-Caminez, was a powerful four-cylinder, air-cooled engine. Vibration problems cut the promising future of this radical engine short.

Flight Setup.

Auto-coordination—Off.

Reality mode—On.

Time: Hours—9. Minutes—30.

Season—Summer.

Surface wind: Knots—37. Degrees—143.

Reliability factor—90.

Only the Airspeed Indicator, Altimeter, Compass, and Artificial Horizon may be used on the Fairchild 24.

Flight Objectives. Fly the Fairchild 24.

Filing the Flight Plan.

Step 1. Start the engine. Full throttle may be used during this flight.

Step 2. Take off from John F. Kennedy International Airport; 17034N 21065E Alt.—12.

Step 3. Climb to an altitude of 3500 feet.

Step 4. Fly to Block Island; 17352N 21749E Alt.—105.

Step 5. Land on runway 10.

Flight Debriefing. You will have successfully completed this flight if you:

☐ Flew the Fairchild 24 to Block Island.

☐ Safely completed the flight.

65. BEECH

Walter Beech entered aviation as a company pilot with the E. M. Laird Company in Wichita, Kansas. His flying exploits enabled him to sell the company's Laird Swallow to several major purchasers during the early 1920s. Disenchantment with the company forced Beech to resign in October 1924. Teaming up with Cessna and Lloyd Stearman, Beech founded the Travel Air Manufacturing Company in Wichita. By 1929, the company had merged with Curtiss-Wright Corporation and Walter Beech was made president of the Curtiss-Wright Travel Air Division.

The nation's financial depression in 1932 forced the Wichita plant to close, with all of the aircraft manufacturing operations being moved to St. Louis, Missouri. Beech's transfer to St. Louis proved to be unsatisfactory and he elected to resign his president position. Determined to make one more attempt at forming a truly successful airplane company, Beech moved back to Wichita and started the Beech Aircraft Corporation. The classic designs created by Beech immediately found a home with the discriminating pilot.

Flight Setup.
Auto-coordination—Off.
Reality mode—On.
Time: Hours—14. Minutes—45.
Season—Winter.
Surface wind: Knots—3. Degrees—32.
Reliability factor—90.
Only the Airspeed Indicator, Altimeter, Compass, and Artificial Horizon may be used on the Beech Bonanza 35.

Flight Objectives. Fly the Beech Bonanza 35.

Filing the Flight Plan.
Step 1. Start the engine. Full throttle may be used during this flight.
Step 2. Take off from Wichita, KS; 15460N 13250E Alt.—1332
Step 3. Climb to an altitude of 7250 feet.
Step 4. Fly to Enid, OK; 14923N 13065E Alt.—1168.
Step 5. Land on runway 17 at Enid.

Flight Debriefing. You will have successfully completed this flight if you:

☐ Flew the Beech Bonanza 35 to Enid, OK.
☐ Safely completed the flight.

66. ROBIN

Several well-known foreign manufacturers have also made an impact on modern civilian aviation. In France, the Centre Est Aéronautique was restructured in 1969 and became the Avions Pierre Robin company. Concentrating on the production of small civilian airplanes from other manufacturers' designs, Robin produced its first "in-house" design in 1967 with the DR.253. Following several modifications, the current DR.400 series retains many of the classic Robin features that were found on the original. Forward-sliding bubble canopies, tricycle landing gear, and low fuselage side walls have become Robin trademarks.

Flight Setup.
Auto-coordination—Off.

Reality mode—On.

Time: Hours—5. Minutes—30.

Season—Fall.

Surface wind: Knots—811. Degrees—111.

Reliability factor—90.

Only the Airspeed Indicator, Altimeter, Compass, and Artificial Horizon may be used on the DR.400.

Flight Objectives. Fly the Robin DR.400.

Filing the Flight Plan.

Step 1. Start the engine. Full throttle may be used during this flight.

Step 2. Take off from Scottsbluff, NE; 17527N 11485E Alt.—3966.

Step 3. Climb to an altitude of 5280 feet.

Step 4. Fly to Rapid City, SD; 18431N 11794E Alt.—3201.

Step 5. Land at Rapid City Regional.

Flight Debriefing. You will have successfully completed this flight if you:

☐ Flew the Robin DR.400 to Rapid City, SD.

☐ Safely completed the flight.

67. MESSERSCHMITT

Following World War II, most of Germany's leading aircraft manufacturing companies were restructured. This arrangement lead to design consortiums in which an aircraft's design is built under a licensing agreement with the original designer. For example, a Swedish designer, Bjorn Andreasson, produced an all-metal airplane with AB Malmö Flygindustri called the MFI-9 Junior. Bolköw Apparatebau of West Germany purchased the license for constructing the Junior in 1961. Two of Germany's more famous wartime manufacturers joined in the production of the Junior, Messerschmitt and Blohm (of Blohm und Voss fame) and the Messerschmitt-Bölkow-Blohm Bö 208C Junior was born.

Flight Setup.

Auto-coordination—Off.

Reality mode—On.

Time: Hours—15. Minutes—00.

Season—Summer.

Surface wind: Knots—31. Degrees—31.

Reliability factor—90.

Only the Airspeed Indicator, Altimeter, Compass, and Artificial Horizon may be used on the Bö 208C.

Flight Objectives. Fly the Bö 208C.

Filing the Flight Plan.

Step 1. Start the engine. Full throttle may be used during this flight.

Step 2. Take off from Boise, ID; 19201N 7774E Alt.—2857.

Step 3. Climb to an altitude of 8000 feet.

Step 4. Fly to Ogden, UT; 17814N 8751E Alt.—4454.

Step 5. Land on runway 3 at Ogden Municipal.

Flight Debriefing. You will have successfully completed this flight if you:

☐ Flew the Bö 208C to Ogden, UT.
☐ Safely completed the flight.

68. GATES LEARJET

Bill Lear made his initial contribution to aviation as a pioneer in aircraft radios during the early 1930s. This modest beginning was eventually acquired by the Siegler Corporation. In the 1950s, Lear's interest swung from aviation electronics to the production of small business jets. Building on the design of the Swiss FFA P-16, Lear formed the Swiss American Aviation Corporation and created the Lear Jet 23. Eventually moving to Wichita, Kansas, Gates Learjet has become recognized as the leader in the production of small business jets. In 1984, the U.S. Air Force elected to lease Gates Learjets as light-duty transports for replacing its aging North American T-39 Sabreliner fleet. Designated C-21As, these Gates Learjets have proved to be economical as well as convenient in their new military role (Fig. 12-2).

Flight Setup.
Auto-coordination—Off.
Reality mode—On.
Time: Hours—8. Minutes—40.
Season—Summer.

Fig. 12-2. This Gates Learjet is designated a C-21A transport when used by the U.S. Air Force.

Cloud layer 1 tops—10,000.
Cloud layer 1 bottoms—4500.
Surface wind: Knots—431. Degrees—181.
Reliability factor—90.
All instrumentation may be used on the Gates Learjet C-21A .
Flight Objectives. Fly the Gates Learjet C-21A.
Filing the Flight Plan.
Step 1. Start the engine. Full throttle may be used during this flight.
Step 2. Take off from Wichita, KS; 15460N 13250E Alt.—1332.
Step 3. Climb to an altitude of 23,000 feet.
Step 4. Fly to Topeka, KS; 15957N 13899E Alt.—1079.
Step 5. Land at Forbes Field, Topeka, KS.
Flight Debriefing. You will have successfully completed this flight if you:

☐ Flew the Gates Learjet C-21A to Topeka, KS.
☐ Safely completed the flight.

69. CESSNA CITATION

Recognizing the potential for the small business jet market, Cessna designed the Cessna Fanjet 500 in October 1968. Following the first flight of the prototype aircraft on 15 September 1969, the jet's name was changed to Cessna Citation. Three different versions of the Citation aircraft line have been produced: the Citation I, II, and III. Basically, the Citation I was the full-production version of the original Citation. The Citation II, which was released in September 1976, had an increased fuselage length and a greater wingspan. These enlargements gave the Citation II a seating capacity of 10 passengers and greater fuel and cargo-carrying ability (Fig. 12-3). Finally, on 30 May 1979, the Citation III, with an even greater capacity, was flown.

Flight Setup.
Auto-coordination—Off.
Reality mode—On.
Time: Hours—7. Minutes—00.
Season—Fall.
Surface wind: Knots—801. Degrees—282.
Reliability factor—90.
All instrumentation may be used on the Cessna Citation III.
Flight Objectives. Fly the Cessna Citation III.
Filing the Flight Plan.
Step 1. Start the engine. Full throttle may be used during this flight.
Step 2. Take off from Wichita, KS; 15460N 13250E Alt.—1332.
Step 3. Climb to an altitude of 9700 feet.
Step 4. Fly to Dodge City, KS; 15610N 12390E Alt.—2594.
Step 5. Land at Dodge City, KS.
Flight Debriefing. You will have successfully completed this flight if you:

☐ Flew the Cessna Citation III to Dodge City, KS.
☐ Safely completed the flight.

Fig. 12-3. The Cessna Citation II. (Photograph courtesy of Cessna Aircraft Company)

70. FALCONJET

Two important features for the small business jet are cabin volume and short-field handling. With reference to the field handling ability of a small jet, taking off and landing on runways that are normally reserved for lightweight piston-powered aircraft increases the flexibility of the business jet. In other words, the jet can be operated from the same type of airport that handles other civilian air traffic.

FalconJets are an exclusive line of business jets which specialize in aircraft with large cabin volumes and superior short-field performance. For example, the Falcon 50, with its three turbofan engines, can travel a distance of 4200 miles, at 459 knots, use an airport with 3000-foot runways, and carry nine passengers with cargo (Fig. 12-4).

Flight Setup.
Auto-coordination—Off.
Reality mode—On.
Time: Hours—18. Minutes—30.
Season—Spring.
Surface wind: Knots—14. Degrees—301.
Reliability factor—90.
All instrumentation may be used on the Falcon 50.
Flight Objectives. Fly the FalconJet Falcon 50.
Filing the Flight Plan.
Step 1. Start the engine. Full throttle may be used during this flight.
Step 2. Take off from Brown Field in San Diego, CA; 14666N 6155E Alt.—525.
Step 3. Climb to an altitude of 35,000 feet.
Step 4. Fly to Santa Catalina VOR; 16003N 5209E Freq.—111.
Step 5. Return to Brown Field and land.

Fig. 12-4. The U.S. Coast Guard uses the FalconJet 200 as a transport aircraft.

Flight Debriefing. You will have successfully completed this flight if you:

☐ Flew the Falcon 50 between San Diego and Santa Catalina.
☐ Safely completed the flight.

71. DOUGLAS

At the other end of the small business jet spectrum are the medium range airliners. These aircraft sacrifice extended range for increased hauling capacity. The jet that started this trend was the Douglas DC-9. Beginning construction on 26 July 1963, the DC-9 was markedly different from the other airliners that were currently in service. The DC-9 was primarily intended as a reliable, short-range transport with a cabin volume for seating 80 passengers. Very few other aircraft manufacturers foresaw the impact that this aircraft would have on the airline industry. Consequently, Boeing was slow to enter this market with its 737 design and lost three years of service to the DC-9.

Delta Air Lines started the first regular DC-9 flights on 8 December 1965. Both private corporations and the U.S. Air Force have also enjoyed the short-range hauling capabilities of the DC-9.

Flight Setup.
Auto-coordination—Off.
Reality mode—On.
Time: Hours—19. Minutes—30.
Season—Summer.
Surface wind: Knots—10. Degrees—286.
Reliability factor—90.
All instrumentation may be used on the DC-9.
Flight Objectives. Fly the Douglas DC-9.
Filing the Flight Plan.
Step 1. Start the engine. Full throttle may be used during this flight.
Step 2. Take off from Albuquerque International Airport; 14782N 9979E Alt.—5353.
Step 3. Climb to an altitude of 10,000 feet.
Step 4. Fly to El Paso International Airport; 13427N 9802E Alt.—3956.
Step 5. Land at El Paso, TX.
Flight Debriefing. You will have successfully completed this flight if you:

☐ Flew a commercial DC-9 from Albuquerque, NM to El Paso, TX.
☐ Safely completed the flight.

72. MODERN NAVIGATION

Cross-country flight has made significant progress since James Knight made his winter flight between Omaha and Chicago. Special aerial navigation equipment fills the cockpit of every civilian aircraft. These instruments help in determining the exact position of the aircraft at any given time during a flight. By knowing this location, the pilot can accurately travel between two points under virtually any weather conditions and in any type of lighting (i.e., day or night).

The two principal instruments used in fixing the position of the aircraft are the VOR (or Omni-Bearing Indicator) and ADF. Additionally, the DME and local airfield beacons also help in establishing the true location of the aircraft.

Flight Setup.
Auto-coordination—Off.
Reality mode—On.
Time: Hours—20. Minutes—45.
Season—Winter.
Surface wind: Knots—5. Degrees—77.
Reliability factor—90.
All instrumentation may be used on the Gates Learjet 25G.
Flight Objectives. Navigate the Gates Learjet 25G at night.
Filing the Flight Plan.
Step 1. Start the engine. Full throttle may be used during this flight.
Step 2. Take off from Las Vegas, NV; 15948N 7236E Alt.—2207.
Step 3. Climb to an altitude of 19,500 feet.
Step 4. Fly to Bryce Canyon; 16278N 8429E Alt.—7587. Use Mormon Mesa (VOR; 16074N

7623E Freq.—114.3) and St. George (VOR; 16140N 7891E Freq.—109.8) for navigation.
   Step 5. Land at Bryce Canyon (VOR; 16275N 8396E Freq.—112.8).
   Flight Debriefing. You will have successfully completed this flight if you:

☐ Navigated between Las Vegas and Bryce Canyon.
☐ Safely completed the flight.

Chapter 13

Aerobatics

73. OUTSIDE LOOP

Flight Setup.
Auto-coordination—Off.
Reality mode—On.
Time: Hours—9. Minutes—00.
Season—Summer.
Reliability factor—90.
All instrumentation may be used during aerobatics.
Flight Objectives. Perform an outside loop.
Filing the Flight Plan.
Step 1. Start the engine and take off. Full throttle may be used during this flight.
Step 2. Climb to 8000 feet.
Step 3. Gain sufficient airspeed, approximately 200 knots.
Step 4. Pitch the aircraft's nose down.
Step 5. Continue to hold the pitch until the aircraft is back to a level flying attitude.
Flight Debriefing. You will have successfully completed this flight if you:

☐ Performed an outside loop.
☐ Safely completed the flight.

74. WINGOVER

Flight Setup.
Auto-coordination—Off.

Reality mode—On.

Time: Hours—9. Minutes—00.

Season—Summer.

Reliability factor—90.

All instrumentation may be used during aerobatics.

Flight Objectives. Perform a wingover.

Filing the Flight Plan.

Step 1. Start the engine and take off. Full throttle may be used during this flight.

Step 2. Climb to 8000 feet.

Step 3. Gain sufficient airspeed, approximately 200 knots.

Step 4. Pitch the aircraft's nose up. Neutralize the pitch.

Step 5. Give a slight amount of aileron roll to the right.

Step 6. Again pitch the nose up. Couple this with a touch of right rudder.

Step 7. Neutralize all controls. You should be heading 180 degress from your beginning position.

Flight Debriefing. You will have successfully completed this flight if you:

☐ Performed a wingover.

☐ Safely completed the flight.

75. SLOW ROLL

Flight Setup.

Auto-coordination—Off.

Reality mode—On.

Time: Hours—9. Minutes—00.

Season—Summer.

Reliability factor—90.

All instrumentation may be used during aerobatics.

Flight Objectives. Perform a slow roll.

Filing the Flight Plan.

Step 1. Start the engine and take off. Full throttle may be used during this flight.

Step 2. Climb to 8000 feet.

Step 3. Gain sufficient airspeed, approximately 200 knots.

Step 4. Give a slight amount of aileron roll to the right and hold.

Step 5. Maintain a true attitude through the corrective use of the rudder and the elevator.

Step 6. Neutralize all controls when the aircraft is level.

Flight Debriefing. You will have successfully completed this flight if you:

☐ Performed a slow roll.

☐ Safely completed the flight.

76. STALL TURN

Flight Setup.

Auto-coordination—Off.

Reality mode—On.

Time: Hours—9. Minutes—00.

Season—Summer.

Reliability factor—90.

All instrumentation may be used during aerobatics.

Flight Objectives. Perform a stall turn.

Filing the Flight Plan.

Step 1. Start the engine and take off. Full throttle may be used during this flight.

Step 2. Climb to 8000 feet.

Step 3. Gain sufficient airspeed, approximately 200 knots.

Step 4. Pitch the nose up into a 90 degree climb. Neutralize the controls.

Step 5. Right before the aircraft begins to stall, move the rudder to the right. Hold the position until the aircraft's nose is pointed towards the ground.

Step 6. Pull out of the dive into a level attitude.

Flight Debriefing. You will have successfully completed this flight if you:

☐ Performed a stall turn.

☐ Safely completed the flight.

77. ROLL OFF THE TOP

Flight Setup.

Auto-coordination—Off.

Reality mode—On.

Time: Hours—9. Minutes—00.

Season—Summer.

Reliability factor—90.

All instrumentation may be used during aerobatics.

Flight Objectives. Perform a roll off the top.

Filing the Flight Plan.

Step 1. Start the engine and take off. Full throttle may be used during this flight.

Step 2. Climb to 8000 feet.

Step 3. Gain sufficient airspeed, approximately 200 knots.

Step 4. Pitch the nose up. Hold this control until the aircraft is inverted. Neutralize the controls at this point.

Step 5. Use full left aileron to roll the aircraft into a level flight attitude.

Flight Debriefing. You will have successfully completed this flight if you:

☐ Performed a roll off the top.

☐ Safely completed the flight.

78. CUBAN EIGHT

Flight Setup.
Auto-coordination—Off.
Reality mode—On.
Time: Hours—9. Minutes—00.
Season—Summer.
Reliability factor—90.
All instrumentation may be used during aerobatics.
Flight Objectives. Perform a Cuban eight.
Filing the Flight Plan.
Step 1. Start the engine and take off. Full throttle may be used during this flight.
Step 2. Climb to 8000 feet.
Step 3. Gain sufficient airspeed, approximately 200 knots.
Step 4. Pitch the nose up. Hold this control until the aircraft is just leaving its inverted attitude. Neutralize the controls at this point.
Step 5. While diving down, roll the aircraft to the right with the ailerons. You will be in a level attitude dive.
Step 6. Again, pitch the nose up and hold as in Step 4.
Step 7. In the inverted dive, roll the aircraft right with the ailerons into a level attitude. At the completion of this maneuver, you will be very near the point where you entered the Cuban eight.
Flight Debriefing. You will have successfully completed this flight if you:

☐ Safely completed the flight.
☐ Performed a Cuban eight.

79. HALF REVERSE CUBAN EIGHT

Flight Setup.
Auto-coordination—Off.
Reality mode—On.
Time: Hours—9. Minutes—00.
Season—summer.
Reliability factor—90.
All instrumentation may be used during aerobatics.
Flight Objectives. Perform a half reverse Cuban eight.
Filing the Flight Plan.
Step 1. Start the engine and take off. Full throttle may be used during this flight.
Step 2. Climb to 8000 feet.
Step 3. Gain sufficient airspeed, approximately 200 knots.
Step 4. Pitch the nose up. Hold this control and use left aileron to roll the aircraft during its climb. You will now be in an inverted attitude. Neutralize the controls at this point.
Step 5. Pitch the nose up (remember, you are inverted; therefore, the nose of the aircraft will dive). Hold this control until you are in a level flight attitude. Neutralize the controls.
Step 6. At the completion of this maneuver you will be facing 180 degrees from the heading where you entered the half reverse Cuban eight.

Flight Debriefing. You will have successfully completed this flight if you:

☐ Performed a half reverse Cuban eight.
☐ Safely completed the flight.

80. BARREL ROLL

Flight Setup.
Auto-coordination—Off.
Reality mode—On.
Time: Hours—9. Minutes-00.
Season—Summer.
Reliability factor—90.
All instrumentation may be used during aerobatics.
Flight Objectives. Perform a barrel roll.
Filing the Flight Plan.
Step 1. Start the engine and take off. Full throttle may be used during this flight.
Step 2. Climb to 8000 feet.
Step 3. Gain sufficient airspeed, approximately 200 knots.
Step 4. Pitch the nose up. Neutralize the control. Use left aileron to roll the aircraft during its climb. You will now be in an inverted and level attitude. Neutralize the control at this point.
Step 5. Pitch the nose up (remember, you are inverted; therefore, the nose of the aircraft will dive). Neutralize the controls. You will now be in an inverted dive.
Step 6. Roll the aircraft with the ailerons. When the aircraft is in a true attitude (i.e., not inverted), level the aircraft with a slight amount of up elevator. You will still be on the same heading as when you entered the maneuver.
Flight Debriefing. You will have successfully completed this flight if you:

☐ Performed a barrel roll.
☐ Safely completed the flight.

81. SQUARE LOOP

Flight Setup.
Auto-coordination—Off.
Reality mode—On.
Time: Hours—9. Minutes—00.
Season—Summer.
Reliability factor—90.
All instrumentation may be used during aerobatics.
Flight Objectives. Perform a square loop.
Filing the Flight Plan.
Step 1. Start the engine and take off. Full throttle may be used during this flight.
Step 2. Climb to 8000 feet.

Step 3. Gain sufficient airspeed, approximately 200 knots.

Step 4. Pitch the aircraft's nose up into a vertical climb and neutralize the control.

Step 5. Prior to stalling, give a large amount of up elevator and place the aircraft into inverted flight.

Step 6. From this level inverted attitude, pitch the nose up into a vertical dive and neutralize the control.

Step 7. Prior to crashing into the ground, pitch the nose up and place the aircraft into a level flight facing on the same heading as the beginning of the maneuver.

Flight Debriefing. You will have successfully completed this flight if you:

☐ Performed a square loop.
☐ Safely completed the flight.

82. VERTICAL ROLL

Flight Setup.
Auto-coordination—Off.
Reality mode—On.
Time: Hours—9. Minutes-00.
Season—Summer.
Reliability factor—90.
All instrumentation may be used during aerobatics.
Flight Objectives. Perform a vertical roll.
Filing the Flight Plan.
Step 1. Start the engine and take off. Full throttle may be used during this flight.

Step 2. Climb to 8000 feet.

Step 3. Gain sufficient airspeed, approximately 200 knots.

Step 4. Pitch the aircraft's nose up into a vertical climb and neutralize the control.

Step 5. Roll the aircraft one-quarter of a turn to the right with aileron. Neutralize the control.

Step 6. Prior to stalling, give a large amount of right rudder and place the aircraft into a dive. Neutralize the rudder control.

Step 7. Roll the aircraft one-quarter of a turn to the right with the aileron. Neutralize the control.

Step 8. Pitch the nose up and place the aircraft in a level attitude. Your heading should be the same as when you began this maneuver.

Flight Debriefing. You will have successfully completed this flight if you:

☐ Performed a vertical roll.
☐ Safely completed the flight.

Appendix A

Annotated Reviews of Flight Simulation Software

The sheer number of flight simulation programs in today's marketplace is indicative of the popularity of this type of software. Very few other genres of software can boast such a large following. This includes entertainment type packages, as well as those used in more profitable business pursuits.

In order to help you better evaluate this enormous aerial offering, all of the major flight simulation software packages have been assembled into this appendix. By definition, "major flight simulation software" refers to those products that can be readily purchased at either a local level or through mail-order companies. Granted, many public domain and independent manufacturers' programs exist, but their long-term availability is unpredictable.

AcroJet

Microprose Software
120 Lakefront Drive
Hunt Valley, MD 21030
(301) 667-1151
Version Tested: Commodore 64 w/64K RAM.
Comments: What is billed as an "advanced flight simulator" turns out to be nothing more than an accelerated version of Solo Flight (see below). With AcroJet, however, you are flying a Bede BD-5J single-seat, lightweight, turbojet-powered aircraft. By using a detached silhouette view of the BD-5J, you fly through 10 boring aerial aerobatic maneuvers.

AIRSIM-3

Mind Systems Corp.
P.O. Box 506
Northampton, MA 01061
(413) 586-6463
Version Tested: Apple //e w/128K RAM.

Comments: With 50 different commands to master, AIRSIM-3 is one of the more powerful flight simulation programs currently available. Poor documentation and the lack of a fuel gauge limit the amount of pleasure that can be derived from this program.

Captain Goodnight and the Islands of Fear

Broderbund Software, Inc.
17 Paul Drive
San Rafael, CA 94903
(415) 479-1170
Version Tested: Apple *IIe* w/128K RAM.
Comments: Captain Goodnight is an extreme departure from all of the other flight simulation software that is mentioned in this appendix. Based loosely on the serial action movies from the 1930s and 1940s, only several "real" flight simulation scenes appear during Captain Goodnight's adventure. The good captain's piloting skills are tested in a high-performance jet fighter, a slow-moving piston-powered transport, and an armed helicopter. In each case, poor flying techniques will result in a crash. If nothing else, Captain Goodnight is an enjoyable diversion from the tense drama of Flight Simulator Action.

Eagles

Strategic Simulations, Inc.
883 Stierlin Road
Building A-200
Mountain View, CA 94043
(415) 964-1200
Versions Tested: Apple *IIe* w/128K RAM and Atari 800XL w/40K RAM.

Flight Simulator and Flight Simulator II

subLOGIC Corporation
713 Edgebrook Drive
Champaign, IL 61830
(217) 359-8482
Versions Tested: Amiga w/256K RAM, Apple *IIe* w/128K RAM, Atari 800XL w/40K RAM, Commodore 64 w/64K RAM, IBM PC XT w/640K RAM, Macintosh w/512K RAM.
Comments: This is the program that started the rush for flight simulation software. None of the other programs discussed in this appendix approach either the complexity or the realism that are present in Flight Simulator and Flight Simulator II.

JET

subLOGIC Corporation
713 Edgebrook Drive
Champaign, IL 61830
(217) 359-8482
Versions Tested: Apple *IIe* w/128K RAM, Commodore 64 w/64K RAM, IBM PC XT w/640K RAM.
Comments: SubLOGIC brings all of the sophistication of Flight Simulator II into the modern jet age. Piloting high-performance versions of the U.S. Air Force's F-16 and U.S. Navy's F/A-18 in numerous tactical and strategic situations form the premise of JET. A companion volume to

162

this book, *JET: 82 Challenging New Adventures* (TAB Book No. 2872), provides detailed instruction for flying this program.

Rendezvous

EDUWare Services, Inc.
185 Berry Street
San Francisco, CA 94107
(415) 546-1937
Version Tested: Apple *IIe* w/128K RAM.
Comments: This is an educational program based on a fictitious space shuttle mission. The low-quality graphics and heavy emphasis on mathematical skills makes this program unattractive for home pilot use.

Skyfox

Electronic Arts
2755 Campus Drive
San Mateo, CA 94403
(415) 571-7171
Version Tested: Apple *IIe* w/128K RAM.
Comments: If you can overlook the fantasy aspects of this program, then you are in for a real ride. Excellent graphics, superb sound, and precision flight characteristics are all prime features of Skyfox. There's even a special arcade game, Alpha Invaders, hidden inside Skyfox. Just trying to discover this secret bonus will be enjoyment enough for some people.

Solo Flight

Microprose Software
120 Lakefront Drive
Hunt Valley, MD 21030
(301) 667-1151
Versions Tested: Apple *IIe* w/128K RAM and IBM PC XT w/640K RAM.
Comments: Solo Flight offers two different methods of simulation. One is a small civilian-type craft that has four different modes of flight: clear weather, landing practice, windy conditions, and IFR. The second simulation is Mail Pilot. Mail Pilot is a game where the computer user must fly the aircraft to various locations carrying differing amounts of mail. Unfortunately, none of your flying, with either method, is from a cockpit perspective. Actually, you're flying an aircraft silhouette several hundred feet in front of your view.

Space Shuttle—A Journey Into Space

Activision
P.O. Box 7287
Mountain View, CA 94039
(800) 227-9759
Version Tested: Apple *IIe* w/128K RAM.
Comments: This is by far the finest space simulation that you will ever fly. All of the sights, sounds, and thrills of flying a space shuttle can be found in this game. Space Shuttle is also supported by some of the best documentation found in flight simulation programming.

Spitfire Simulator

Mind Systems Corp.
P.O. Box 506
Northampton, MA 01061
(413) 586-6463
Version Tested: Apple IIe w/128K RAM.
Comments: If you can overlook the minimal documentation, vector graphics, and the odd positioning for the joystick, then Spitfire Simulator will take you into the wild blue yonder of the skies over England during the Battle of Britain. Takeoffs, landings, fuel consumption, and Messerschmitts—it's all available in Spitfire Simulator.

Stunt Flyer

Sierra Online
P.O. Box 485
Coatsegold, CA 93614
Version Tested: Commodore 64 w/64K RAM.
Comments: Several nice features make this modest flight simulator worth a careful look. There are three choices for flight: air show, free flight, and stunt flying. The stunt flying option presents the greatest attraction with Stunt Flyer. After selecting your stunt from a menu, you take to the air and execute your selection. Following your attempt, a special replay feature shows your performance from a ground observer's vantage point. Unfortunately, the poor graphics and awful sound negate many of the pluses found in Stunt Flyer.

Super Huey

Cosmi, Inc.
415 N. Figueroa Street
Wilmington, CA 90744
Version Tested: Commodore 64 w/64K RAM.
Comments: Four different graphic scenarios taken from the cockpit of a Super Huey helicopter. Both the rescue and combat missions generate the greatest degree of excitement. Both the graphics and sound capabilities of the Commodore 64 are realistically exploited in Super Huey.

Tranquility Base

EDUWare Services, Inc.
185 Berry Street
San Francisco, CA 94107
(415) 546-1937
Version Tested: Apple IIe w/128K RAM.
Comments: Tranquility Base tests your skill at flying a NASA Lunar Excursion Module (LEM) around America's first lunar colony. This program's intended education scope stresses the physics of gravitation and motion. Therefore, users after a more thrilling bit of flight simulation, should consider piloting one of the other programs listed in this appendix instead of becoming lost in space at Tranquility Base.

Miscellaneous

Ace of Aces by Accolade Software.
B-1 Nuclear Bomber by Avalon Hill Software.
Beach Head by Access Software.

Beachhead II by Access Software.
The Dam Busters by Accolade.
50 Mission Crush by Strategic Simulations, Inc.
Hellcat Ace by Microprose Software.
Jet Combat Simulator by Epyx Software.
Jump Jet by Avant-Garde Creations.
Raid Over Moscow by Access Software.
Spitfire Ace by Microprose Software.
Spitfire '40 by Avalon Hill Software.
Zaxxon by Datasoft, Inc.

Comments: There are numerous games that function in the environment of a flight simulation situation. These games offer a great degree of excitement, usually, at the expense of realism.

Appendix B

Writing Your Own Flight Simulation Program

This appendix contains complete computer program listings, for several popular personal microcomputer types, describing a simple flight simulator. Each of these programs is written in the elementary computer language, BASIC (Beginner's ALL-purpose Symbolic Instruction Code). No special provisions will be necessary for running these programs. Only the keyboard and the standard amount of memory inherent to each particular computer type is required.

Begin by typing in the program *exactly* as it appears in the listing that matches your brand of computer. Any deviations from the listing could result in a "crushed" computer. Make sure that the computer's Caps Lock key is engaged during this program entry stage. Since an introduction into computer programming is beyond the scope of this appendix, all explanatory remark statements have been removed form each program listing. Believe me, if you type the program into your computer exactly as it is printed in these listings, it will work properly. Trust me.

Once you have entered the complete program listing, double-check your typing. Catching an error at this time will prevent disappointments later. Now save the program on a suitable medium. This step must be performed before your first "test flight." Assign the name FLY ME to your saved BASIC program file.

Seven basic flight control actions are simulated in this program: level flight, climb, dive, bank-left, bank-right, landing gear operation, and weapons launching. The keyboard keys for performing these actions are:

```
N = normal flight
M = climb
I = dive
J = bank-left
K = bank-right
```

G = landing gear Up/Down
F = weapons launch
S = stop

Each of these keyboard commands requires an upper case key entry. Therefore, the computer's Caps Lock key must be depressed during operation of FLY ME. In order to retain the highest degree of realism, always begin and end all of your flight maneuvers from the normal flight attitude. Figure B-1 shows FLY ME in a normal flight attitude. Failure to follow this simple rule will result in some rather ridiculous flight patterns. For example:

Normal Flight

Inverted Flight

Bank-Left and -Right

The Right Way;
A loop—Press M three times; M + M + M
The Wrong Way;
A loop—press M followed by N three times; M + N + M + N + M + N
The major benefit of FLY ME is its rendering of a detached visual accounting of the basic aircraft controls used in Flight Simulator. By working with this short program, you will develop a better understanding of the forces that are being exerted on your aircraft as you exercise a specific aerial maneuver. Of course, after you have mastered FLY ME, you can add some of your own programming for simulating actual takeoffs and landings.

Listing B-1. FLY ME for the Apple II family of computers.

```
5   HOME
10  G = 0:I = 0:M = 0:J = 0:K$ = " "
20  HGR
30  POKE  - 16302,0
40  HCOLOR= 3
50  HPLOT 100,100 TO 120,100
60  HPLOT 103,99 TO 120,99
```

```
70    HPLOT 103,101 TO 120,101
80    HPLOT 108,98
90    HPLOT 118,97 TO 120,97
100    HPLOT 117,98 TO 120,98
110    HPLOT 120,96
120 P =  PEEK ( - 16336)
130 K =  PEEK ( - 16384)
140  IF K > 127 THEN  GOTO 200
150  GOTO 120
200   GET K$
210  IF K$ = "N" THEN  GOTO 20
220  IF K$ = "S" THEN  TEXT : END
230  IF K$ = "M" THEN  GOTO 300
240  IF K$ = "I" THEN  GOTO 400
250  IF K$ = "J" THEN  GOTO 500
260  IF K$ = "K" THEN  GOTO 500
270  IF K$ = "G" THEN  GOTO 600
280  IF K$ = "F" THEN  GOTO 700
290  IF K$ <  > "N" OR K$ <  > "S" OR K$ <  > "I" OR K$ <  > "M" OR K$ <
      > "J" OR K$ <  > "K" OR K$ <  > "G" OR K$ <  > "F" THEN  GOTO 120
300 I = I + 1
302   HGR
304  IF I = 2 THEN  GOTO 330
306  IF I = 3 THEN  GOTO 350
308  IF I = 4 THEN I = 0: GOTO 20
310   HPLOT 105,85 TO 120,100
312   HPLOT 108,87 TO 120,99
314   HPLOT 107,88 TO 119,100
316   HPLOT 113,90
318   HPLOT 118,96 TO 121,99
320   HPLOT 120,97 TO 122,99
322   HPLOT 122,98
324   GOTO 120
330   HGR
332   HPLOT 120,80 TO 120,100
334   HPLOT 119,83 TO 119,100
336   HPLOT 121,83 TO 121,100
338   HPLOT 122,88
340   HPLOT 122,97 TO 122,100
342   HPLOT 123,98 TO 123,100
344   HPLOT 124,100
346   GOTO 120
350   HGR
352   HPLOT 120,100 TO 140,100
354   HPLOT 120,99 TO 137,99
356   HPLOT 120,101 TO 137,101
358   HPLOT 132,102
360   HPLOT 120,102 TO 123,102
362   HPLOT 120,103 TO 122,103
364   HPLOT 120,104
366   GOTO 120
400 M = M + 1
402   HGR
404  IF M = 2 THEN  GOTO 430
406  IF M = 3 THEN  GOTO 350
408  IF M = 4 THEN M = 0: GOTO 20
410   HPLOT 105,115 TO 120,100
412   HPLOT 108,113 TO 120,101
```

```
414    HPLOT 107,112 TO 119,100
416    HPLOT 110,108
418    HPLOT 116,102 TO 119,99
420    HPLOT 117,100 TO 119,98
422    HPLOT 118,98
424    GOTO 120
430    HGR
432    HPLOT 120,100 TO 120,120
434    HPLOT 119,100 TO 119,117
436    HPLOT 121,100 TO 121,117
438    HPLOT 118,112
440    HPLOT 118,100 TO 118,103
442    HPLOT 117,100 TO 117,102
444    HPLOT 116,100
446    GOTO 120
500    HGR
501 J = J + 1
502    IF J = 2 THEN  GOTO 530
504    IF J = 3 THEN  GOTO 550
506    IF J = 4 THEN  GOTO 570
508    IF J = 5 THEN  GOTO 530
509    IF J = 6 THEN J = 0: GOTO 20
510    HPLOT 100,100 TO 120,100
511    HPLOT 103,99 TO 120,99
512    HPLOT 103,101 TO 120,101
513    HPLOT 108,98 TO 119,98
514    HPLOT 110,97 TO 119,97
515    HPLOT 112,96 TO 119,96
516    HPLOT 114,95 TO 119,95
517    HPLOT 116,94 TO 119,94
518    HPLOT 118,93 TO 119,93
519    HPLOT 108,102 TO 119,102
520    HPLOT 110,103 TO 119,103
521    HPLOT 112,104 TO 119,104
522    HPLOT 114,105 TO 119,105
523    HPLOT 116,106 TO 119,106
524    HPLOT 118,107 TO 119,107
525    GOTO 120
530    HGR
531    HPLOT 115,100 TO 130,100
532    HPLOT 119,97 TO 119,100
533    HPLOT 126,97 TO 126,100
534    HPLOT 122,99 TO 123,99
535    GOTO 120
550    HGR
551    HPLOT 120,100 TO 140,100
552    HPLOT 120,99 TO 137,99
553    HPLOT 120,101 TO 137,101
554    HPLOT 132,98
555    HPLOT 120,98 TO 123,98
556    HPLOT 120,97 TO 122,97
557    HPLOT 120,96
558    GOTO 120
570    HGR
571    HPLOT 120,100 TO 140,100
572    HPLOT 120,99 TO 137,99
573    HPLOT 120,101 TO 137,101
574    HPLOT 121,98 TO 132,98
```

```
575   HPLOT 121,97 TO 130,97
576   HPLOT 121,96 TO 128,96
577   HPLOT 121,95 TO 126,95
578   HPLOT 121,94 TO 124,94
579   HPLOT 121,93 TO 122,93
580   HPLOT 121,102 TO 132,102
581   HPLOT 121,103 TO 130,103
582   HPLOT 121,104 TO 128,104
583   HPLOT 121,105 TO 126,105
584   HPLOT 121,106 TO 124,106
585   HPLOT 121,107 TO 122,107
586   GOTO 120
600   HGR
601 G = G + 1
602   IF G = 2 THEN G = 0: GOTO 20
604   HPLOT 100,100 TO 120,100
606   HPLOT 103,99 TO 120,99
608   HPLOT 103,101 TO 120,101
610   HPLOT 108,98
612   HPLOT 118,97 TO 120,97
614   HPLOT 117,98 TO 120,98
616   HPLOT 120,96
618   HPLOT 104,102 TO 104,103
620   HPLOT 112,102 TO 112,103
622   GOTO 120
700   HGR
702   HPLOT 100,100 TO 120,100
704   HPLOT 103,99 TO 120,99
706   HPLOT 103,101 TO 120,101
708   HPLOT 108,98
710   HPLOT 118,97 TO 120,97
712   HPLOT 117,98 TO 120,98
714   HPLOT 120,96
716   PRINT  CHR$ (7)
720   FOR X = 1 TO 99
722   HPLOT 100 - X,101 TO 103 - X,101
724 P =  PEEK ( - 16336)
726   HCOLOR= 0
728   HPLOT 100 - X,101 TO 103 - X,101
730   HCOLOR= 3
732   NEXT X
734   GOTO 120
```

Listing B-2. FLY ME for the IBM PC family of computers.

```
10 KEY OFF
20 G=0:I=0:M=0:J=0:K$=""
30 CLS:SCREEN 1:COLOR ,1
40 LINE (100,100)-(120,100)
50 LINE (103,99)-(120,99)
60 LINE (103,101)-(120,101)
70 PSET (108,98)
80 LINE (118,97)-(120,97)
90 LINE (117,98)-(120,98)
100 PSET (120,96)
110 SOUND 40,.1
120 K$=INKEY$
130 IF K$="" THEN 110
```

```
200 IF K$="N" THEN 30
210 IF K$="S" THEN KEY ON:SCREEN 0:WIDTH 80:END
220 IF K$="M" THEN 300
230 IF K$="I" THEN 400
240 IF K$="J" THEN 500
250 IF K$="K" THEN 500
260 IF K$="G" THEN 600
270 IF K$="F" THEN 700
280 IF K$<>"N" OR K$<>"S" OR K$<>"I" OR K$<>"M" OR K$<>"J" OR K$<>"K" OR
    K$<>"G" OR K$<>"F" THEN 110
300 I=I+1
302 CLS
304 IF I=2 THEN 330
306 IF I=3 THEN 350
308 IF I=4 THEN I=0:GOTO 30
310 LINE (105,85)-(120,100)
312 LINE (108,87)-(120,99)
314 LINE (107,88)-(119,100)
316 PSET (112,90)
318 LINE (118,96)-(121,99)
320 LINE (120,97)-(122,99)
322 PSET (122,98)
324 GOTO 110
330 CLS
332 LINE (120,80)-(120,100)
334 LINE (119,83)-(119,100)
336 LINE (121,83)-(121,100)
338 PSET (122,88)
340 LINE (122,97)-(122,100)
342 LINE (123,98)-(123,100)
344 PSET (124,100)
346 GOTO 110
350 CLS
352 LINE (120,100)-(140,100)
354 LINE (120,99)-(137,99)
356 LINE (120,101)-(137,101)
358 PSET (132,102)
360 LINE (120,102)-(123,102)
362 LINE (120,103)-(122,103)
364 PSET (120,104)
366 GOTO 110
400 M=M+1
402 CLS
404 IF M=2 THEN 430
406 IF M=3 THEN 350
408 IF M=4 THEN M=0:GOTO 30
410 LINE (105,115)-(120,100)
412 LINE (108,113)-(120,101)
414 LINE (107,112)-(119,100)
416 PSET (110,108)
418 LINE (116,102)-(119,99)
420 LINE (117,100)-(119,98)
422 PSET (118,98)
424 GOTO 110
430 CLS
432 LINE (120,100)-(120,120)
434 LINE (119,100)-(119,117)
436 LINE (121,100)-(121,117)
```

```
438 PSET (118,112)
440 LINE (118,100)-(118,103)
442 LINE (117,100)-(117,102)
444 PSET (116,100)
446 GOTO 110
500 CLS
501 J=J+1
502 IF J=2 THEN 530
504 IF J=3 THEN 550
506 IF J=4 THEN 570
508 IF J=5 THEN 530
509 IF J=6 THEN J=0:GOTO 30
510 LINE (100,100)-(120,100)
511 LINE (103,99)-(120,99)
512 LINE (103,101)-(120,101)
513 LINE (108,98)-(119,98)
514 LINE (110,97)-(119,97)
515 LINE (112,96)-(119,96)
516 LINE (114,95)-(119,95)
517 LINE (116,94)-(119,94)
518 LINE (118,93)-(119,93)
519 LINE (108,102)-(119,102)
520 LINE (110,103)-(119,103)
521 LINE (112,104)-(119,104)
522 LINE (114,105)-(119,105)
523 LINE (116,106)-(119,106)
524 LINE (118,107)-(119,107)
525 GOTO 110
530 CLS
531 LINE (115,100)-(130,100)
532 LINE (119,97)-(119,100)
533 LINE (126,97)-(126,100)
534 LINE (122,99)-(123,99)
535 GOTO 110
550 CLS
551 LINE (120,100)-(140,100)
552 LINE (120,99)-(137,99)
553 LINE (120,101)-(137,101)
554 PSET (132,98)
555 LINE (120,98)-(123,98)
556 LINE (120,97)-(122,97)
557 PSET (120,96)
558 GOTO 110
570 CLS
571 LINE (120,100)-(140,100)
572 LINE (120,99)-(137,99)
573 LINE (120,101)-(137,101)
574 LINE (121,98)-(132,98)
575 LINE (121,97)-(130,97)
576 LINE (121,96)-(128,96)
577 LINE (121,95)-(126,95)
578 LINE (121,94)-(124,94)
579 LINE (121,93)-(122,93)
580 LINE (121,102)-(132,102)
581 LINE (121,103)-(130,103)
582 LINE (121,104)-(128,104)
583 LINE (121,105)-(126,105)
584 LINE (121,106)-(124,106)
```

```
585 LINE (121,107)-(122,107)
586 GOTO 110
600 CLS
601 G=G+1
602 IF G=2 THEN G=0:GOTO 30
604 LINE (100,100)-(120,100)
606 LINE (103,99)-(120,99)
608 LINE (103,101)-(120,101)
610 PSET (108,98)
612 LINE (118,97)-(120,97)
614 LINE (117,98)-(120,98)
616 PSET (120,96)
618 LINE (104,102)-(104,103)
620 LINE (112,102)-(112,103)
622 GOTO 110
700 CLS
702 LINE (100,100)-(120,100)
704 LINE (103,99)-(120,99)
706 LINE (103,101)-(120,101)
708 PSET (108,98)
710 LINE (118,97)-(120,97)
712 LINE (117,98)-(120,98)
714 PSET (120,96)
716 BEEP
720 FOR X=1 TO 99
722 LINE (100-X,101)-(103-X,101),3
724 SOUND 110,.2
726 LINE (100-X,101)-(103-X,101),0
728 NEXT X
730 COLOR ,1
732 GOTO 110
```

Listing B-3. FLY ME for the Macintosh computer.

```
CLS
G=0:I=0:M=0:J=0:K$=""
NORMAL:
 CLS
    LINE (100,100)-(120,100),33
    LINE (103,99)-(120,99)
    LINE (103,101)-(120,101)
    PSET (108,98)
    LINE (118,97)-(120,97)
    LINE (117,98)-(120,98)
    PSET (120,96)
KEYCHECK:
 SOUND 40,1
 K$=INKEY$
    IF K$="" THEN KEYCHECK
    IF K$="N" THEN NORMAL
    IF K$="S" THEN CLS:END
    IF K$="M" THEN UP
    IF K$="I" THEN DOWN
    IF K$="J" THEN BANK
    IF K$="K" THEN BANK
    IF K$="G" THEN GEAR
    IF K$="F" THEN FIRE
        IF K$<>"N" OR K$<>"S" OR K$<>"I" OR K$<>"M" OR K$<>"J" OR K$<>"K" OR K$<>"G"
    OR K$<>"F"
```

```
    THEN KEYCHECK
UP:
 I=I+1
 CLS
  IF I=2 THEN UPII
  IF I=3 THEN UPIII
  IF I=4 THEN I=0:GOTO NORMAL
       LINE (105,85)-(120,100)
       LINE (108,87)-(120,99)
       LINE (107,88)-(119,100)
       PSET (112,90)
       LINE (118,96)-(121,99)
       LINE (120,97)-(122,99)
       PSET (122,98)
       GOTO  KEYCHECK
UPII:
 CLS
       LINE (120,80)-(120,100)
       LINE (119,83)-(119,100)
       LINE (121,83)-(121,100)
       PSET (122,88)
       LINE (122,97)-(122,100)
       LINE (123,98)-(123,100)
       PSET (124,100)
       GOTO KEYCHECK
UPIII:
 CLS
       LINE (120,100)-(140,100)
       LINE (120,99)-(137,99)
       LINE (120,101)-(137,101)
       PSET (132,102)
       LINE (120,102)-(123,102)
       LINE (120,103)-(122,103)
       PSET (120,104)
       GOTO KEYCHECK
DOWN:
 M=M+1
 CLS
  IF M=2 THEN DOWNII
  IF M=3 THEN UPIII
  IF M=4 THEN M=0:GOTO NORMAL
       LINE (105,115)-(120,100)
       LINE (108,113)-(120,101)
       LINE (107,112)-(119,100)
       PSET (110,108)
       LINE (116,102)-(119,99)
       LINE (117,100)-(119,98)
       PSET (118,98)
       GOTO KEYCHECK
DOWNII:
 CLS
       LINE (120,100)-(120,120)
       LINE (119,100)-(119,117)
       LINE (121,100)-(121,117)
       PSET (118,112)
       LINE (118,100)-(118,103)
       LINE (117,100)-(117,102)
       PSET (116,100)
```

174

```
        GOTO KEYCHECK
BANK:
 CLS
 J=J+1
     IF J=2 THEN BANKII
     IF J=3 THEN BANKIII
     IF J=4 THEN BANKIV
     IF J=5 THEN BANKII
     IF J=6 THEN J=0:GOTO NORMAL
         LINE (100,100)-(120,100)
         LINE (103,99)-(120,99)
         LINE (103,101)-(120,101)
         LINE (108,98)-(119,98)
         LINE (110,97)-(119,97)
         LINE (112,96)-(119,96)
         LINE (114,95)-(119,95)
         LINE (116,94)-(119,94)
         LINE (118,93)-(119,93)
         LINE (108,102)-(119,102)
         LINE (110,103)-(119,103)
         LINE (112,104)-(119,104)
         LINE (114,105)-(119,105)
         LINE (116,106)-(119,106)
         LINE (118,107)-(119,107)
         GOTO KEYCHECK
BANKII:
 CLS
     LINE (115,100)-(130,100)
     LINE (119,97)-(119,100)
     LINE (126,97)-(126,100)
     LINE (122,99)-(123,99)
     GOTO KEYCHECK
BANKIII:
 CLS
     LINE (120,100)-(140,100)
     LINE (120,99)-(137,99)
     LINE (120,101)-(137,101)
     PSET (132,98)
     LINE (120,98)-(123,98)
     LINE (120,97)-(122,97)
     PSET (120,96)
     GOTO KEYCHECK
BANKIV:
 CLS
     LINE (120,100)-(140,100)
     LINE (120,99)-(137,99)
     LINE (120,101)-(137,101)
     LINE (121,98)-(132,98)
     LINE (121,97)-(130,97)
     LINE (121,96)-(128,96)
     LINE (121,95)-(126,95)
     LINE (121,94)-(124,94)
     LINE (121,93)-(122,93)
     LINE (121,102)-(132,102)
     LINE (121,103)-(130,103)
     LINE (121,104)-(128,104)
     LINE (121,105)-(126,105)
     LINE (121,106)-(124,106)
```

```
        LINE (121,107)-(122,107)
        GOTO KEYCHECK
GEAR:
 CLS
 G=G+1
  IF G=2 THEN G=0:GOTO NORMAL
    LINE (100,100)-(120,100)
    LINE (103,99)-(120,99)
    LINE (103,101)-(120,101)
    PSET (108,98)
    LINE (118,97)-(120,97)
    LINE (117,98)-(120,98)
    PSET (120,96)
    LINE (104,102)-(104,103)
    LINE (112,102)-(112,103)
    GOTO KEYCHECK
FIRE:
 CLS
    LINE (100,100)-(120,100),33
    LINE (103,99)-(120,99)
    LINE (103,101)-(120,101)
PSET (108,98)
LINE (118,97)-(120,97)
LINE (117,98)-(120,98)
PSET (120,96)
 BEEP
FOR X=1 TO 99
    LINE (100-X,101)-(103-X,101),33
      SOUND 910,1
    LINE (100-X,101)-(103-X,101),0
NEXT X
 GOTO KEYCHECK
```

Appendix C

Aircraft Identification Guide

This appendix provides illustrations and performance specifications for many of the aircraft discussed in the Historical Aviation Scenarios found in Part II of this book.

Name: 182G Skylane.
Manufacturer: Cessna Aircraft Company.
Powerplant: Continental 180-horsepower engine.
Performance: 146 knots at 14,900 feet.
Dimensions: Wingspan, 36 feet; length, 28 feet.
Weight: Empty, 1752lb; loaded, 3100lb.

Fig. C-1. Cessna 182G Skylane. (courtesy Cessna Aircraft Company)

Name: Wright 1903 Flyer.
Manufacturer: Wright Brothers.
Powerplant: Custom/Wright 12-horsepower engine.
Performance: 5.9 knots at 10 feet.
Dimensions: Wingspan, 40 feet 4 inches; length, 21 feet 3/8 inch.
Weight: Empty, 605lb; loaded, 760lb.

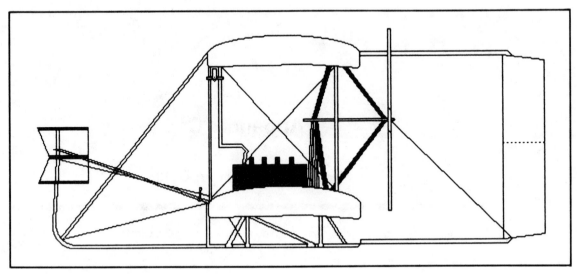

Fig. C-2. Wright 1903 Flyer.

Name: Type XII.
Manufacturer: Bleriot.
Powerplant: Anzani 25-horsepower engine.
Performance: 40.5 knots 20,000 feet.
Dimensions: Wingspan, 25 feet 7 inches; length, 26 feet 3 inches.
Weight: Empty, 463lb; loaded, 661lb.

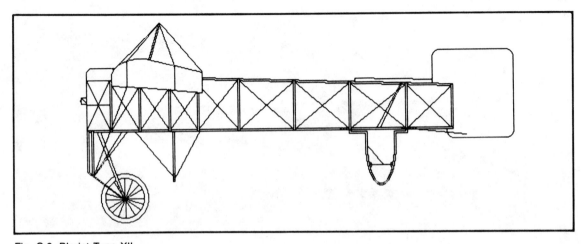

Fig. C-3. Bleriot Type XII.

Name: N.
Manufacturer: Morane-Saulnier.
Powerplant: Le Rhône 110-horsepower engine.
Performance: 83 knots at 10,000 feet.
Dimensions: Wingspan, 27 feet 3 inches; length, 22 feet.
Weight: Empty, 735lb; loaded, 1122lb.

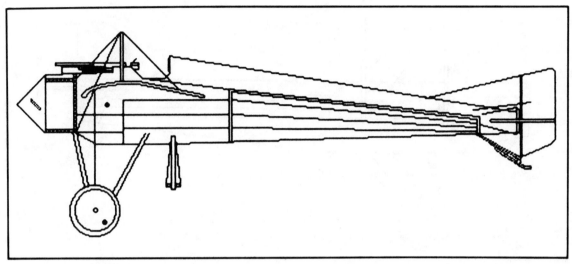

Fig. C-4. Morane-Saulnier N.

Name: E-III.
Manufacturer: Fokker Aeroplanbau.
Powerplant: Oberursel 80-horsepower engine.
Performance: 76 knots at 9800 feet.
Dimensions: Wingspan, 32 feet 8 inches; length, 23 feet 6 1/2 inches.
Weight: Empty, 878lb; loaded, 1342lb.

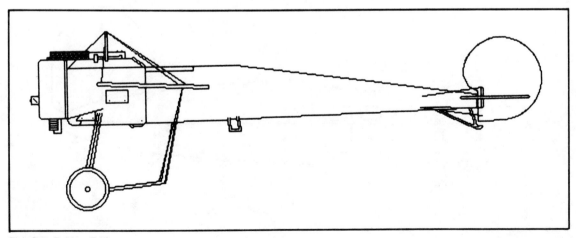

Fig. C-5. Fokker E-III.

Name: M-2.
Manufacturer: Douglas.
Powerplant: Liberty 400-horsepower engine.
Dimensions: Wingspan, 39 feet 8 inches; length, 28 feet 11 inches.
Weight: Empty, 2910lb; loaded, 4968lb.

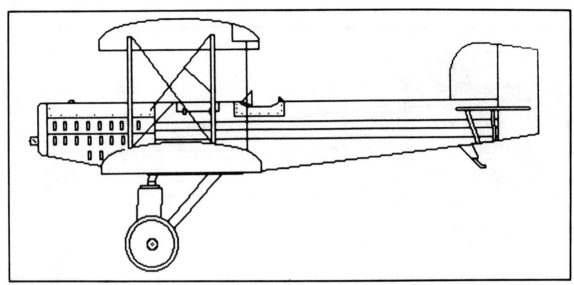

Fig. C-6. Douglas M-2.

Name: 5B Vega.
Manufacturer: Lockheed.
Powerplant: Pratt and Whitney 450-horsepower engine.
Dimensions: Wingspan, 41 feet; length, 27 feet 6 inches.
Weight: Empty, 1650lb; loaded, 3200lb.

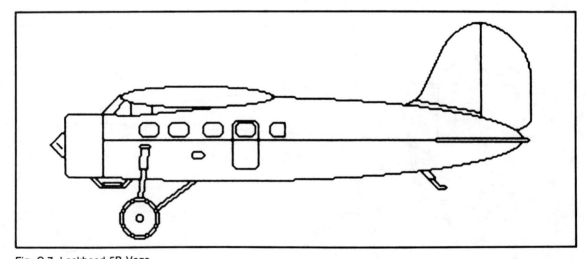

Fig. C-7. Lockheed 5B Vega.

Name: 5C Vega.
Manufacturer: Lockheed.
Powerplant: Pratt & Whitney 500-horsepower engine.
Dimensions: Wingspan, 41 feet; length, 27 feet 6 inches.
Weight: Empty, 2595lb; loaded, 4500lb.

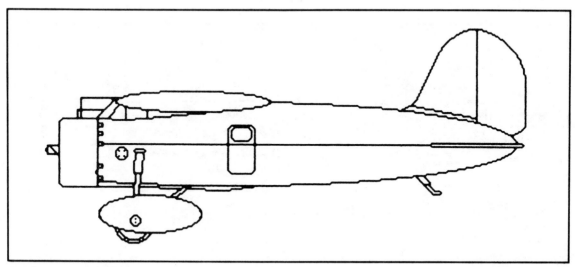

Fig. C-8. Lockheed 5C Vega.

Name: XP-6A.
Manufacturer: Curtiss.
Powerplant: Curtiss Conqueror 600-horsepower engine.
Dimensions: Wingspan, 31 feet 6 inches; length, 23 feet 2 inches.
Weight: Empty, 2699lb; loaded, 3392lb.

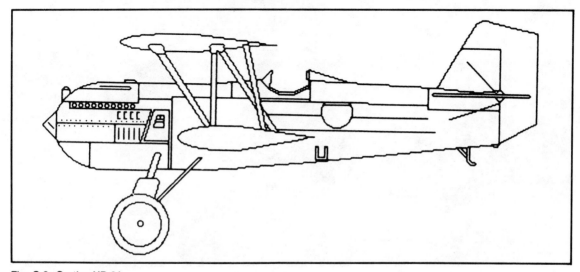

Fig. C-9. Curtiss XP-6A.

Name: Bf 110C-1.
Manufacturer: Bayerische Flugzeugwerke A.G.
Powerplant: Two Daimler-Benz engines each rated at 1100 horsepower.
Performance: 292 knots at 32,800 feet.
Dimensions: Wingspan, 53 feet 3 inches; length, 39 feet 7 inches.
Weight: Empty, 9755lb; loaded, 13,289lb.

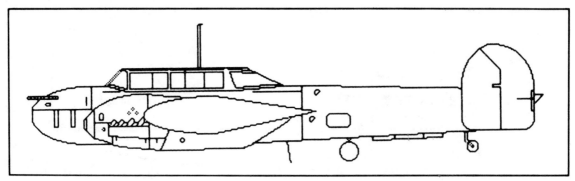

Fig. C-10. Messerschmitt Bf 110C.

Name: P-40E.
Manufacturer: Curtiss.
Powerplant: Allison 1150-horsepower engine.
Dimensions: Wingspan, 37 feet 4 inches; length, 31 feet 2 inches.
Weight: Empty, 6350lb; loaded, 8280lb.

Fig. C-11. Curtiss P-40E.

Name: B-25C-20.
Manufacturer: North American.
Powerplant: Two Wright engines each rated at 1700 horsepower.
Performance: 236 knots at 24,200 feet.
Dimensions: Wingspan, 67 feet 7 inches; length, 52 feet 11 inches.
Weight: Empty, 21,100lb; loaded, 35,000lb.

Fig. C-12. North American B-25.

Name: P-51D.
Manufacturer: North American.
Powerplant: Packard/Merlin 1695-horsepower engine.
Performance: 380 knots at 25,000 feet.
Dimensions: Wingspan, 37 feet; length, 32 feet 3 inches
Weight: Empty, 7125lb; loaded, 12,100lb.

Fig. C-13. North American P-51D.

Name: B-17G.
Manufacturer: Boeing.
Powerplant: Four Wright engines each rated at 1200 horsepower.
Performance: 260 knots at 37,500 feet.
Dimensions: Wingspan, 103 feet 9 inches; length, 74 feet 9 inches.
Weight: Empty, 34,000lb; loaded, 72,100lb.

Fig. C-14. Boeing B-17G.

Name: A6M Reisen (An A6M replica is pictured.)
Manufacturer: Mitsubishi.
Powerplant: Sakae 1130-horsepower engine.
Dimensions: Wingspan, 36 feet 1 inch; length, 29 feet 11 inches.
Weight: Empty, 4136lb; loaded, 6025lb.

Fig. C-15. Mitusbishi A6M Reisen replica (converted T-6).

Name: B-29A.
Manufacturer: Boeing.
Powerplant: Four Wright engines each rated at 2200 horsepower.
Performance: 313 knots at 35,000 feet.
Dimensions: Wingspan, 141 feet 2 inches; length, 99 feet.
Weight: Empty, 90,000lb; loaded, 120,000lb.

Fig. C-16. Boeing B-29A.

Name: 140.
Manufacturer: Cessna Aircraft Company.
Powerplant: Continental C85 85-horsepower engine.
Dimensions: Wingspan, 30 feet; length, 20 feet.
Weight: Empty, 800lb; loaded, 1200lb.

Fig. C-17. Cessna 140. (courtesy Cessna Aircraft Company)

186

Name: PA-18.
Manufacturer: Piper Aircraft Corporation.
Powerplant: Avco Lycoming 150-horsepower engine.
Performance: 113 knots at 19,000 feet.
Dimensions; Wingspan, 35 feet 2 inches; length, 22 feet 7 inches.
Weight: Empty, 983lb; loaded 1750lb.

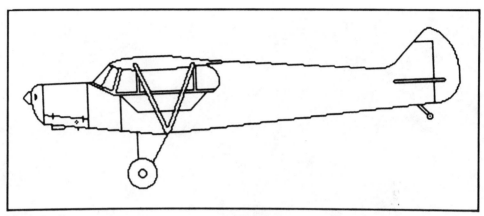

Fig. C-18. Piper PA-18.

Name: V35B.
Manufacturer: Beech Aircraft Corporation.
Powerplant: Continental 285-horsepower engine.
Performance: 182 knots at 17,800 feet.
Dimensions: Wingspan, 33 feet 6 inches; length, 26 feet 5 inches.
Weight: Empty, 2117lb; loaded, 3400lb.

Fig. C-19. Beech V35B. Photograph courtesy of Beech Aircraft Corporation.

187

Name: 25G.
Manufacturer: Gates Learjet Corporation.
Powerplant: Two General Electric engines each rated at 2950lb thrust.
Performance: 464 knots at 45,000 feet.
Dimensions: Wingspan, 35 feet 7 inches; length, 47 feet 7 inches.
Weight: Empty, 8250lb; loaded, 16,300lb.

Fig. C-20. Gates Learjet 25. Photograph courtesy of Gates Learjet Corporation.

Name: Citation II.
Manufacturer: Cessna Aircraft Company.
Powerplant: Two Pratt & Whitney engines each rated at 2500lb thrust.
Performance: 385 knots at 43,000 feet.
Dimensions: Wingspan, 51 feet 8 inches; length, 47 feet 2 inches.
Weight: Empty, 7181lb; loaded, 13,300lb.

Fig. C-21. Cessna Citation II (courtesy Cessna Aircraft Company).

Appendix D

An Aviation Time Line

The following chronology represents significant events in aviation history.

1894

First successful glider flights by Otto Lilienthal.

1896

May 6: Samuel Pierpont Langley's steam-powered aircraft makes its first engine-driven flight.
August 10: Otto Lilienthal dies from injuries received from a glider crash.

1903

December 17: Wilbur and Orville Wright make their historic flight near Kitty Hawk, North Carolina.

1907

November 7: $25,000 is allocated by the Signal Corps for the purchase of an airplane.
December 5: Wilbur Wright makes a bid for the $25,000 Signal Corps contract.

1908

February 10: The Wright Brothers receive the first Army airplane contract.
May 14: The first passenger ride in a Wright Brothers aircraft is made at Kitty Hawk.
August 12: Lighter-than-air airship test flights are officially conducted at Ft. Meyer, Virginia.
September 17: Lt. Thomas Selfridge becomes the first to be killed in an airplane crash.

1909

January 23: Louis Bleriot becomes the first person to fly across the English Channel in an airplane.

July 27: A new two-man flight endurance record is set—1 hour, 12 minutes, 40 seconds.

July 30: The Wright Brothers' Army aircraft completes a 10-mile cross-country flight.

August 2: The Army formally accepts the Wright Brothers aircraft.

October 26: Lt. F. Humphreys is the first Army pilot to solo.

1910

August 8: Tricycle landing gear is first installed on an aircraft.

September 23: George Chavez flies over the Swiss Alps, but is killed in a landing mishap.

October 11: Theodore Roosevelt becomes the first President to fly in an airplane.

1911

January 21: Radio-telephonic transmission from a moving aircraft is achieved by the Army.

March 17: The Signal Corps purchases its first Curtiss airplane.

July: Harriet Quimby becomes the first woman pilot in the United States.

September 19: Aerial photographic experiments are conducted from a moving aircraft.

1912

February 17: Pilot physical examination requirements are established by the Army.

April 16: Harriet Quimby is the first woman to fly across the English Channel.

May 6: Three Army airplanes complete the first cross-country flight.

June 7-8: Captain Charles Chandler mounts a machine gun on an airplane.

September 28: Corporal Frank S. Scott is the first enlisted man to die in an airplane crash.

1914

January 1: Tony Jannus pilots the first scheduled airline flight. He flies between Tampa and St. Petersburg, Florida.

February 16: Lts. Carberry and Taliaferro set the Army altitude record with a height of 8,700 feet.

June 28: Archduke Francis Ferdinand and his wife Sophie are assassinated.

July 28-October 30: World war erupts over the Ferdinand assassination. World War I begins.

1915

May 7: The liner *Lusitania* is sunk by a torpedo.

1918

February 28: President Wilson signs a law requiring pilots to obtain a license.

April 14: Alan Winslow and Douglas Campbell score the first American aerial combat "kills."

April 21: Manfred von Richthofen, the "Red Baron," is killed.

April 29: Lt. Edward Rickenbacker shoots downs his first enemy aircraft.

May 15: Continuously scheduled airmail service between New York City, Philadelphia, and Washington, D.C. is started.

November 10: The last American patrol is flown over enemy lines during World War I.

November 11: The Armistice is signed; World War I ends.

1919

April 19: A nonstop flight record is set from Chicago to New York.
May 19: M/Sgt. R. Bottriell makes the first parachute jump.
September 24: A passenger plane sets an altitude record of 30,900 feet.
October 30: The reversible pitch propeller is tested.
November 10: Regular international airmail service between London and Paris is started.

1921

February 22-23: James Knight flies the first night airmail run from Omaha, Nebraska, to Chicago, Illinois.

1924

April 6-September 28: The United States fields the first air team to fly around the world.

1926

May 9: Richard E. Byrd and Floyd Bennett fly over the North Pole.

1927

May 20-21: Charles Lindbergh completed the first solo flight over the Atlantic in the *Spirit of St. Louis*.
May 25: Lt. James Doolittle performs the first outside loop.

1929

August 8-29: The airship *Graf Zeppelin* becomes the first lighter-than-air craft to fly around the world.
September 30: Fritz von Opel flies the first rocket-powered plane.
November 28-29: Richard E. Byrd and three others fly over the South Pole.

1931

September 18: The Japanese invade Manchuria.

1932

May 20-21: Amelia Earhart becomes the first woman to fly nonstop across the Atlantic.
August 24-25: Amelia Earhart becomes the first woman to fly nonstop across the United States.

1933

July 15-22: Wiley Post becomes the first person to fly around the world solo.

1934

February 9: The Army assumes all domestic airmail duties.
June 1: The Army stops performing domestic airmail duties.
June 28: Boeing receives contract for building the B-17.

1935

January 11-12: Amelia Earhart makes the first female solo flight between Hawaii and California.

August 15: Wiley Post and Will Rogers die in a floatplane crash near Point Barrow, Alaska.
September 13: Howard Hughes sets a world speed record of 352.322 mph in his Hughes H-1 airplane.

1936

June 25: American Airlines begins nonstop New York-to-Chicago passenger flights.

1937

Amelia Earhart is lost over the Pacific Ocean during the final leg of her world flight attempt.
January 19: Howard Hughes sets a new transcontinental speed record in the Hughes H-1.

1939

June 24: Harold Gray pilots the first transatlantic airmail flight.
September 1: Germany invades Poland. World War II begins.

1941

December 7: Japan attacks Pearl Harbor in Hawaii.
December 8: The United States declares war on Japan.
December 20: The Flying Tigers begin air operations against the Japanese.

1942

April 18: Col. James Doolittle bombs Tokyo with 16 B-25s.
April 28: Flying Tiger pilots destroy 22 Japanese aircraft in one mission.
July 4: The B-17 makes its first arrival for combat in the European Theater of Operations.

1944

March 6: 600 Allied bombers attack Berlin.
June 6: 15,000 sorties are flown by Allied aircraft in support of the D-Day Invasion.
June 13: German V-1 rockets begin exploding in London.

1945

March 9: 300 B-29 bombers fire-bomb Tokyo and destroy 25 percent of the city.
March 11: 1,079 Allied aircraft bomb Essen, Germany.
March 18: 1,920 aircraft attack Berlin.
April 10: German Me262 jet fighters shoot down 10 Allied bombers over Berlin.
August 6: *Enola Gay* drops the first atomic bomb on Hiroshima.
August 9: *Bocks Car* drops the second atomic bomb on Nagasaki.
September 2: Japan surrenders. World War II ends.

1947

October 14: Captain C. Yeager breaks the sound barrier in the X-1.

1948

June 26: The Berlin Airlift begins.

1949

April 16: Over 12 tons of food are delivered at the height of the Berlin Airlift.
May 12: The Russian blockade of West Berlin ends.
September 30: The Berlin Airlift ends.

1950

June 25: The Korean War begins.
November 8: The first jet-versus-jet combat occurs.

1953

July 27: The Korean War ends.
September 1: Two jets make the first aerial refueling connection.
November 20: A. Crossfield flies a Douglas D-558-2 at twice the speed of sound.

1955

June 29: The B-52 bomber enters the Air Force arsenal.

1958

May 31: The last SAC B-36 is retired. (This is the only U.S. bomber up to this time never to have fired a shot or dropped a bomb in combat.)

1959

January 22: The USAF reveals that less than one percent of all UFO sightings can be classified as unknown.

1961

January 1: U.S. advisors are sent to South Vietnam.
August 13: East German soldiers begin construction of the Berlin Wall.

1962

March 21: A bear survives a supersonic aircraft ejection seat test.

1963

May 18: Jacqueline Cochran becomes the first woman to fly faster than the speed of sound.
October 7: Gates Learjet makes the first flight of their new jet line with a Model 23 prototype.

1965

February 7: The United States' major involvement in Vietnam begins.
June 18: B-52 bombers begin operations in the Vietnam War.
July 10: The USAF scores its first air combat kill during the Vietnam War.

1966

March 4: USAF F-4C jets engage MiG-17 jets in aerial combat over North Vietnam.
April 12: B-52 bombers make their first strike against North Vietnam.

April 26: Maj. P. Gilmore and Lt. W. Smith score the first "kill" of a MiG-21 over North Vietnam.

1967

October 3: Major William Knight sets a world speed record of 4,534 mph in the X-15.

1968

January 31: The ill-fated North Vietnamese Tet Offensive begins.

February 2: 60,000 Viet Cong and North Vietnamese regulars surround the U.S. Marine base at Khe Sanh.

February 24: United States forces regain the territory lost during the Tet Offensive. North Vietnam suffers over 30,000 casualties.

July 5: U.S. Marines are withdrawn from Khe Sanh.

1969

February 9: The Boeing 747 makes its first flight.

March 2: The world's first supersonic civilian aircraft, the Concorde, completes its maiden flight.

July 1: The 2,500th rescue mission during the Vietnam War is performed by an Aerospace Rescue and Recovery team.

July 20: A human lands on the moon. Neil Armstrong becomes the first human to set foot on the moon's surface.

1972

May: Over 11,000 mines are air-dropped into Haiphong harbor and other vital North Vietnamese waterways.

1973

January 27: A peace agreement is signed between the United States and North Vietnam.

July 18: The United States finishes the removal of mines from North Vietnamese waters.

1976

July 28: An SR-71A piloted by Capt. Eldon Joersz and Maj. George Morgan, Jr. sets a speed record of 2,193.17 mph.

1977

February 18: A modified Boeing 747 carries the Space Shuttle Orbiter *Enterprise* above its fuselage from Edwards AFB to Florida.

August 23: Taking a giant step backwards, the *Gossamer Condor* makes the first man-powered aircraft flight with Bryan Allen as pilot.

1986

December 23: Dick Rutan and Jeanna Yeager end a nine-day flight in *Voyager*, becoming the first to fly around the world nonstop and unrefueled.

Glossary

AAA—Antiaircraft artillery.

AAM—Air-to-air missile.

ace—A term applied to a pilot who scores a minimum of five aerial kills.

ACM—Air Combat Maneuvering, a U.S. Navy term for dogfighting.

ACT—Air Combat Tactics, a U.S. Air Force term for dogfighting.

ADF—Automatic Direction Finder.

AGL—Above Ground Level, or aircraft altitude above the ground.

AGM—Air-to-ground missile.

air-to-ground—An aerially initiated ground strike.

airfoil—A lift-producing shape.

ailerons—Control surfaces for banks and rolls.

altimeter—An altitude measuring instrument which commonly reads the atmospheric pressure for determining the aircraft's current height.

ARM—Anti-radiation missile.

ATC—Air Traffic Control.

ATIS—Automatic Terminal Information Service.

bail out—*See* punch out.

bandit—A common U.S. pilot term for an enemy aircraft.

bank—A roll maneuver.

bearing—A horizontal direction indication.

bogey—An unidentified approaching aircraft.

bolter—Missing the arresting cable of an aircraft carrier during landing.

break—A high-performance turn.

burner—Slang term for a jet's afterburner.

buster—Slang term for 100 percent engine power exclusive of afterburner.

CAG—Carrier Air Group Commander.
CAP—Combat Air Patrol.
ceiling—The altitude of the lowest portion of the present cloud layer.
chord—The width of the wing from its leading edge to its trailing edge.
clock—Location positions relative to the aircraft's orientation that are presented in terms of the numeric values on an analog clock face, e.g., 12 o'clock is straight ahead and 6 o'clock is the airplane's tail.
com—Radio communication.
cruising altitude—An altitude that is maintained during level flight.

deck—The minimal altitude of the current ground cover.
density altitude—An adjusted altitude with reference to a fixed standard atmospheric altitude.
dihedral—The upward angle of a lifting surface.
DME—Distance Measuring Equipment.
DOD—Department of Defense.
drag—The frictional force created by the aircraft moving through the air.

ECM—Electronic countermeasures.
elevator—Control surface for upward and downward pitch.
ETA—Estimated time of arrival.
ETD—Estimated time of departure.
ETE—Estimated time enroute.

FAA—Federal Aviation Administration.
FAC—Forward Air Controller.
flak—The aerial bomb burst from an AAA shell.
flaps—A movable surface for increased lift and drag.
fox—A coded radio signal for an air-to-air missile launch.

GCI—Ground-controlled intercept; a ground-based target identification system.
ground speed—The speed of the aircraft relative to the ground.

heading—the compass direction that the aircraft is currently traveling.
HF—High Frequency.
HSI—Horizontal Situation Indicator.
HUD—Head-Up Display.
hypergolic—Compounds that ignite on contact with each other.

IAF—Initial Approach Fix.
IAS—Indicated airspeed.
IFR—Instrument Flight Rules.
ILS—Instrument Landing System.
INS—Inertial Navigation System.
ITT—Inlet turbine temperature.

jinking—A defensive air maneuver, randomly altering an aircraft's heading and altitude.

kill—The destruction of an intended target.
knots—Nautical miles per hour.

LF—Low Frequency.
LOC—Localizer, the horizontal guidance subsystem of the ILS.

Mach—A ratio of true airspeed and the speed of sound; Mach 1 equals 760 mph at sea level.
mayday—An international distress call.

NAS—Naval Air Station.
NATO—North Atlantic Treaty Organization.
nautical mile—*See* nm.
nav—Navigation radio.
navaid—A navigational ground station which transmits VOR or NDB.
NDB—Nondirectional beacon.
NFO—Naval Flight Officer; exclusive of the pilot.
nm—Nautical mile; equals 6076.115 feet or 1852 meters.

OBI—Omni-Bearing Indicator.
OBS—Omni-Bearing Selector.
overshoot—A faster offensive aircraft suddenly moving in front of the target aircraft. This places the offensive aircraft in a defensive posture.

pitch—The upward and downward movement of an aircraft's nose.
pitot-static tube—An external air pressure sensor.
punch out—Emergency ejection from an aircraft.

rate of climb—A feet per minute measurement of the aircraft's current climb rate.
RIO—Radar Intercept Officer; a non-pilot aircrew member. A U.S. Navy term.
RMI—Radio Magnetic Indicator.
RNAV—Area navigation.
ROE—Rules of engagement; predetermined criteria for engaging the enemy.
roll—Horizontal axis rotation.
rotate—The point where the nosewheel leaves the runway during takeoff.
rpm—Revolutions per minute.

SAC—Strategic Air Command.
SAM—Surface-to-air missile.
SID—Standard Instrument Departure.
six—A slang term for the tail position of an aircraft, i.e., 6 o'clock.
skid—A slide out of a turn.
slip—A sideways drop out of a turn.
sortie—A single aerial mission of one aircraft.
STAR—Standard Terminal Arrival Route.

TAS—True airspeed.
TCA—Terminal Control Area.
Top Gun—A U.S. Navy air combat training school at Miramar NAS, California.
touch-and-go—A simulated landing approach.
transceiver—A radio that is able to both transmit and receive signals.
transponder—Enhances the aircraft's radar reflection.
trim—Small adjustment surfaces found on the major control surfaces.
true airspeed—An aircraft's real speed through the air with reference to undisturbed air.
turn and bank indicator—Displays the aircraft's current attitude.

VFR—Visual Flight Rules.
VHF—Very High Frequency.
VHF—Very Low Frequency.
VNAV—Vertical Navigation.
VOR—Very High Frequency Omnidirectional Radio Range.
VSI—Vertical Speed Indicator; also rate of climb indicator.

waypoint—An RNAV-generated VOR.
WSO—Weapons System Officer; a non-pilot aircrew member. A U.S. Air Force term.

yaw—Vertical axis rotation.
yoke—The control stick or joystick.
yo-yo—A vertical defensive aerial combat maneuver.

Index

Other Best Sellers From TAB

☐   **C PROGRAMMING—WITH BUSINESS
APPLICATIONS—Dr. Leon A. Wortman
and Thomas O. Sidebottom**

This learn-by-doing guide puts its emphasis on actual programs that demonstrate the ways C code is entered, manipulated, and modified to achieve specific applications goals. Also included are sample runs for many of the programs and a disk containing all of the book's programs, for use on the !BM PC/XT/AT and compatibles with at least 256K. 260 pp., 95 illus.

Paper $18.95   **Hard $25.95**
Book No. 2857

☐   **TURBO PASCAL® TOOLBOX—A Programmer's
Guide—Paul Garrison**

In this FIRST and ONLY in-depth look at the Turbo modules, veteran computer author Paul Garrison gives you the data you need to decide which of the Turbo Pascal toolbox modules offer the programming features you need, and how to make full use of the modules once you make your purchase. Writing in clear, easy-to-follow style, he includes over **200 example programs, procedures, and subroutines** on topics ranging from word processing and database handling to color graphics and games. 288 pp., 207 illus.

Paper $17.95   **Hard $25.95**
Book No. 2852

☐   **WORKING WITH SUPERCALC® 4—Jerry Willis
and William Pasewark**

Up-to-date instructions for using new SuperCalc 4 to organize and manage data for business and financial applications. Now IBM® PC and compatible users can quickly organize, arrange, and manipulate all types of information using the new and vastly improved SuperCalc 4, one of the top software packages on the market today! This comprehensive guide shows you how to use this powerful electronic spreadsheet for all your own personal applications needs. Packed with applications data and actual example programs! 300 pp., 125 illus.

Paper $18.95   **Hard $24.95**
Book No. 2814

☐   **FRAMEWORK II™ APPLICATIONS—2nd Edition
—Richard H. Baker**

This invaluable, revised edition shows you how to get the most out of Framework II's vastly improved communications facilities, its strengthened word processor, and its larger spreadsheet. And you'll learn how to do most of it by direct command using one of Framework's unique functions called "Idea Processing." This feature allows you to think about information as you do naturally, instead of trying to conform to the needs of your computer. 336 pp., 218 illus.

Paper $19.95   **Hard $26.95**
Book No. 2798

☐   **C PROGRAMMER'S UTILITY LIBRARY
—Frank Whitsell**

Here's a sourcebook that goes beyond simple programming techniques to focus on the efficient use of system resources to aid in the development of higher quality C programs! It's a unique collection of ready-to-use functions and utilities! There's also a ready-to-run disk available for use on the IBM PC/XT/AT and compatibles with at least 256K. 200 pp., 268 illus.

Paper $16.95   **Hard $24.95**
Book No. 2855

☐   **MICROCOMPUTER APPLICATIONS
DEVELOPMENT: TECHNIQUES FOR EVALUATION AND
IMPLEMENTATION—Michael Simon Bodner,
and Pamela Kay Hutchins**

This comprehensive guide represents an overview of the process of application development in the microcomputer environment from BOTH a technical methodology and a business issues point of view. The authors introduce the steps involved in applications development: as well as numerous shortcuts and development tips that they have learned over the years. You'll get invaluable insight into the various types of projects you may encounter. 256 pp., 69 illus.

Hard $24.95   **Book No. 2840**

☐   **dBASE III® PLUS: ADVANCED APPLICATIONS
FOR NONPROGRAMMERS—Richard H. Baker**

The new dBASE III PLUS makes all the advantages offered by dBASE as a programming language incredibly easy even for the non-programmer. And to make it even simpler for you to program like a pro, dBASE expert Richard Baker leads you painlessly through each programming step. Focusing on the practical rather than the theoretical aspects of programming, he explores dBASE III PLUS on three levels—entry level, intermediate, and experienced. 448 pp., 232 illus.

Paper $19.95   **Hard $27.95**
Book No. 2808

☐   **MAXIMUM PERFORMANCE WITH LOTUS® 1-2-3®,
Versions 1.0 and 2.0—Robin Stark and Stuart Leitner**

Going far beyond the material covered in ordinary user's manuals, the authors provide expert techniques, shortcuts, and programming tips gleaned from their own experience and the experience of others who have reached "power-user" status in 1-2-3 operation. Included are "10 tricks every Lotus user should know" and "10 common worksheet problems and how to solve them!" 250 pp., 96 illus.

Paper $17.95   **Hard $25.95**
Book No. 2771

Other Best Sellers From TAB